THE APPRECIATION OF THE ARTS 9

General Editor : Harold Osborne

The Appreciation of
Stained Glass

the appreciation of the arts 9

THE APPRECIATION OF
STAINED GLASS *Lawrence Lee*

London · *Oxford University Press* · New York · Toronto · 1977

Oxford University Press, Walton Street, Oxford OX2 6DP
OXFORD LONDON GLASGOW NEW YORK
TORONTO MELBOURNE WELLINGTON CAPE TOWN
IBADAN NAIROBI DAR ES SALAAM LUSAKA ADDIS ABABA
KUALA LUMPUR SINGAPORE JAKARTA HONG KONG TOKYO
DELHI BOMBAY CALCUTTA MADRAS KARACHI

ISBN 0 19 211913 3

British Library Cataloguing in Publication Data
Lee, Lawrence, b. 1909
    The appreciation of stained glass.—(The
    appreciation of the arts; 9)
    ISBN 0–19–211913–3
    1. Title 2. Series
    748.5   NK5304
    Glass painting and staining

*Printed in Great Britain by
Hazell Watson & Viney Ltd. Aylesbury. Bucks*

CONTENTS

Illustrations

Photographs which have no acknowledgement are the copyright of the author.

When I was watching man's first landing on the moon's surface, it came as a shock to me to realize that there could be no stained glass on the moon, at least, not in the form we have understood it in the past. For, if we imagine a chapel set down on the moon and ourselves inside looking out through its stained glass windows, all we should see would be black space with, possibly, a part of the horizon brilliantly lit at the base, this alone showing the colours and painting of the glass; the rest would have only the faintest reflection from nearby sunlit objects. The effect would be similar to that of a window lit artificially from outside at night, where the source of light is seen as a 'flare spot' (as photographers call it) and the rest of the window is left in relative darkness. Thus we only have the art we are about to define because the light of the sun is diffused by a layer of atmosphere enveloping the earth's surface. When we say that the life of windows is light we ought rather to say that their life is atmosphere, since that is the medium on which our apprehension of light depends. In space, once having left its source in the sun, light is to all intents invisible until it strikes some solid body, so that the astronaut is brightly lit by the sun unless he moves into the shadow say, of the lunar module, when he becomes practically invisible.

The civilizing influence of glass is taken for granted 'It is a little thing, glass is, that is until there isn't any.'[1] Glass transforms with crystalline planes the openings that man has provided to allow light into his shelters, making possible the creation of specialized environments. In these glazed openings he puts signals to inform the traveller: flowers (this is a home), goods (this is a shop). The most potent transformation is brought about by the use of stained glass— those fragile curtains of colour and imagery remaining with us from the past, and continuing to be made in those parts of the world where there still prevails a notion of a god who came to give light and who is mysteriously its source. Whether you call this myth, tribal magic, or sound metaphysics, there is no doubt that it has been the first sanction and definition of the art of arranging coloured glass. Though

All Saints, North Street, York. Detail from 'Prick of Conscience' window. 15th century.

---

[1] Mark Twain, *A Connecticut Yankee at the Court of King Arthur.*

Otaniemi, Finland, Technical University chapel. A clear glazed opening exploiting a natural background.

we shall go on to define stained glass in more material terms, this purpose must never be forgotten.

Stained glass, in strictly technical terms can be described as an assemblage of variously coloured pieces of glass supported in a single flat plane by leads and fixed more or less permanently in a frame of stone, wood, or metal; the design being expressed partly by the arrangement of the shapes of glass and leads, and partly by the addition of glass paint and stains rendered impervious to erasure by being fired into the surface of the glass before leading-up (or glazing). Its essential form is two-dimensional, non-tactile mostly monumental in scale and placed (normally) in non-utilitarian buildings for the purpose of assisting the creation of a special atmosphere as required by a particular cult. For the purpose of this definition, decorative or artistic glass in secular buildings is deemed to be furthering the 'cults' of banking, municipal government, air travel, education, and so forth.

The intention of this book is to assist an active appreciation of

English stained glass. The following chapters are, therefore, an intensive briefing for what one hopes will be a long and enjoyable field study. The subject has an advantage over most other major arts for, compared with them, the 'field' is not large geographically nor are the specimens to be found overwhelming in number. The analogy of a field study is not inappropriate, since the objects of its study are well spread over the area and many metaphorical stones must be lifted to find small but important fragments in the scattered pattern. The student will not be much concerned with concentrations in art galleries, museums, or famous collections, but with abbeys, great and small parish churches, out-of-the-way chapels, public buildings, and private houses. There are no comprehensive lists of these places,[1] few of them have guides or catalogues which give anything more than the barest facts; at times you may be confronted with a window of historic or artistic importance about which there is no information at all. Though the literature of stained glass is not large, there does not seem to be a published bibliography and by far the greater proportion of books are concerned with archaeological and historic aspects of schools, styles, and techniques—all very useful when the time comes and special interests are aroused.

Although we shall be concerned mainly with English stained glass, it is important to remember that the making of coloured windows had its beginning on the continent of Europe. So far as we can judge from the fragmentary evidence, it began somewhere near the heart of the Carolingian Empire and developed first in Germany and then in neighbouring countries as an already mature craft of leaded and painted glass. Styles were at first severely monumental in common with the Romanesque idiom in mosaic and sculpture, and later, with the flowering of thirteenth-century art and architecture, the images took on the gently flowing sophistry of the Gothic age. The Gothic style is usually reckoned to have started with the building of a new choir in the Abbey Church of St. Denis near Paris under the inspired guidance of the Abbé Suger. His great desire for lightness through enlarged windows set masons on a path of stone engineering which a century later reached its natural goal in the 'chapel of glass' of

---

[1] There is an organization called Corpus Vitrearum Medii Aevi. Composed of scholars and scientists, it is preparing an inventory of all the historic stained glass in Europe which may take over thirty years to complete.

Wissembourg, France. Head of Christ, 11th–12th century. Said to be the earliest painted glass extant.

Sainte-Chapelle; it almost overreached itself at Beauvais in one of the loftiest of all cathedrals. From the Île-de-France the emphasis passed to Chartres where its special manifestation of corporate devotion after the destruction of an earlier church seems to have been responsible for a new cathedral of outstanding beauty of architecture, sculpture, and stained glass. We now see a great creative flush spreading from north west France marked successively by great ranges of windows in Bourges, Le Mans, Tours, Sens, Poitiers, Auxerre, followed by many other cathedrals and abbeys throughout northern France, and

Canterbury Cathedral,
Martyrdom window
(detail). 13th century.

the Low Countries. By virtue of the existence of Christendom's 'Common Market', the same creative spirit came to England very early, and notably to Canterbury. It should not be forgotten that Canterbury Cathedral was originally a Romanesque building (in England called Norman) before, in later times, it was enlarged to the predominantly Gothic building we see today.

The widening circle spreading from the Franco-German nucleus reached Italy and Spain in the fourteenth century, and each showed characteristics of its own, the latter owing much to its subject Flemish provinces. In Italy the new naturalism of Giotto influenced glass painters and they acquired a strong interest in the expression of three-dimensional depth and a more natural light and shade (chiaroscuro) in their figures and backgrounds. With the growth in political importance of the Low Countries vigorous schools of glass painting grew and spread all over the Protestant north, including England, where the iconoclastic zeal of the Reformation had reduced the glaziers' craft to the status of a depressed trade.

Arguments still go on as to whether the first glaziers at Canterbury were French or English—they were probably both—but very soon, we can be sure, native schools grew up and were responsible for the

bulk of the original glass in, say, York, Norwich, or Wells. If the common culture of Christendom in force during the first two or three centuries of English glass had persisted to the present day, there would be a certain irrelevance about the phrase 'English stained glass', for though from the start individual schools and styles could be recognized—this from southern Germany, that from north western France, and so on—a common religion and official language made it very easy for skilled labour to be sent anywhere that new building demanded. Art historians get very bothered about whether a twelfth-century fragment at York suggests French influence or if some glass in Normandy was painted by an Englishman, but it really doesn't matter. After all, in those times a French bishop might occupy an English see or an Englishman a French one, indeed Chartres itself once had an English bishop.

Much has been written about the origin of the designs which glaziers used. There seems to be no doubt that in most instances these would have been supplied by the illuminators who already had a complete knowledge of the required iconography and a great facility in designing images to be contained in given shapes.[1] But the problem of how the first use of coloured glass developed into the assured technique apparent in the earliest known examples of any size, namely the well-known windows at Augsburg, will probably remain unsolved.

There are therefore places in the terrain where the sun of high aesthetics has not penetrated—partly, one suspects, because of the thickets of medievalism, sentimentality, or actual technical difficulties peculiar to stained glass. Here the writer, being a practising glazier, will guide with a lantern over a known path.

The suggestion of gloom may seem odd when the essence of our subject is light but it is not entirely unsuitable to the image conjured up in many minds at the words 'stained glass', nor is it unfitting as we look back through the long shadow between the recent past and the

[1] See G. G. Coulton's introduction to *Stained Glass of the XII & XIII Centuries for French Cathedrals* by M. Aubert (Batsford) for a vivid picture of the life of the medieval craftsman.

Barbarossa and his sons, from German Chronicles of the 12th century.

far, bright, late medieval landscape. There is some confusion too. The very phrase 'stained glass' is a stumbling block, for we have a great art form described by words which relate only to one part of its process. Indeed, if by 'stained' one means the application of silver oxide to white glass to give a yellow colour, there are many windows in which this is quite absent; on the other hand if the word 'stained' means the basic colouring of the molten glass—the point at which colour 'strikes' or becomes fused—'coloured glass' would be a more apt description. But it is still rather like describing painting as 'painted canvas' or sculpture as 'wrought stone'. The term 'stained glass' seems to have come into use around the beginning of the nineteenth century as a contraction of 'painted and stained glass'; in the Middle Ages it was simply called 'glass' or 'glaziers' work'; in Germany it is 'Glasmalerei' and in France 'vitrail'. However, 'stained glass' has become a term in our language and to try to change it would only add to the confusion.

The ambiguity of nomenclature reflects another difficulty—how we think about the people who make stained glass windows. Are they artists, as painters and sculptors are artists? Before the sixteenth century this question would not have been asked. In the language of architects they were all—painters, sculptors, glaziers—simply specialist sub-contractors to the main contractor—or in business parlance, servants of the company, more or less equal in status. We can best answer the question by asking another. Assuming we asked a reasonably well-read layman, to whom names like Sutherland, Moore, and Picasso are immediately familiar, to mention an artist well known for his windows, could he name one? He might think of names such as Piper, Chagall, or Léger, but all these were already established as painters (and continue to be thought of as such) before they became involved in designing for stained glass. The same must be said of Matisse, Manessier, and Rouault, though the last did in fact begin his career in a stained glass studio. There are many artists working in stained glass in Britain, France, Germany, and America producing windows for all manner of important buildings, some of their work being in the very latest idioms of modern art, often revolutionary in technique; yet their names are not only unknown to the public in general but not even immediately familiar to art experts, critics, or proprietors of art galleries. This anonymity of artists in stained glass illustrates one more of the difficulties to be overcome if we are to achieve a reasonably straight entry into the appreciation of our subject. We shall deal with the matter in a more positive way in Chapter 3, but for the moment the problem can be underlined by the fact that there are artists known to the author who, though earning their living by the practice of stained glass, prefer

Assy. Window by
Georges Rouault.

for reasons of prestige to be known as painters or sculptors.

The basic function of stained glass as a protection against the elements imposes another condition on our study to which we must become accustomed. This is the condition that public architecture is the inescapable environment of stained glass. Paintings and sculptures have come off the wall and been hidden from the stare of common man in the hot-house of the art gallery. Not so with glass. Apart from fragments in museums or private houses, all coloured and painted windows are in more or less public buildings performing their essential practical function of keeping out weather and letting in light. The indispensable sub-contract to the main contractor is still the glaziers' and will remain so until we all live in plastic domes, in which case the glazier may claim the right to be the main contractor. Therefore you must not say 'Have you seen the John Piper at Coventry?' or 'the Marc Chagall at Tudeley?', but rather 'I am going to see the Baptistery window in the modern cathedral at Coventry' or 'the east window in the ancient village church at Tudeley'. These windows stand or fall by their proper or improper existence in those particular buildings. Whatever complexities are met with in the field, this primary function is one factor to which you must always refer.

With equal certainty we shall encounter the phenomenon of religion, and (another of those limitations) only one religion, namely Christianity.

Almost all the subject matter of windows is Christian propaganda, sometimes true and noble, sometimes bogus and mean, and our examination will not be complete unless we try to develop some personal judgement on these values. One must assume that those who are violently antipathetic to religion in general or to Christianity in particular will not be interested in stained glass; but there are many who, tolerant of most forms of religious creativity, yet feel that their subject matter is of secondary importance to their formal or aesthetic value as works of art. It is rather as we used to judge the formal beauty of Greek sculpture without much reference to or knowledge of the mythology which created a certain concept of gods and goddesses. In this introduction all that need be said is that, though for convenience we have a separate chapter on subject matter,[1] all the mythology, symbolism, images, in fact the whole theology of Christianity, are integral to the formal intention of church windows and cannot be dissociated from them without damage to under-standing. Just as the theologian must take into account the enormous effect which artists of all kinds have had on the definition of the notion of God, conversely, the artist must acknowledge the elegant

---

[1] See p. 98 and following.

formulas of theologians as a framework and inspiration for visual images. This is, of course, understood by most thinking people today in a rather intellectual way, but the full implications for the artist often remain unrecognized or, being unpalatable and unfashionable, are simply ignored.

We have drifted back to current conceptions of the artist in order to strike a cautionary note about how we should think of artists engaged in work which is primarily religious in its genesis. At this level of activity there must of necessity be a tension between each man's individual ego and a kind of collective psyche, a holding down of himself and a lifting up of his fellow beings; the private image manifested in the public place with skill and subtlety, and, above all, with a special kind of humility. By this standard we shall learn to condemn with equal severity those windows which are merely massive exercises in self-expression and those which, even more blasphemously, offer a cheap stereotyped religious picture.

It would be an impertinence to think the reader guilty of the fallacy of seeing windows as little more than pictures which happen to be transparent; but true appreciation could yet be clouded by an unconscious reference to the criteria of painting. Even after instruction in the harsh facts of function, structure, and iconography we may falter in our assessment of a particular window and fall back on those inbred principles by which we have learnt to judge fine art. By fine art is meant, in this context, those generally accepted models of free creativity in painting and sculpture whose expression of plastic values has been analysed, set down, and become implicit in all our discussions of art, that is, the work of artists. It may not be easy for some to learn that much intrinsic beauty and some special faults in windows will be overlooked or miscalculated if the above standard only is applied. Another and more precise instrument is needed, one which is clinically sensitive, for instance, to a range of values in colour phenomena which are quite specific to the medium of glass. For you cannot apply instruments of analysis that deal only with opaque surface and the illusions built up on that surface to the things which happen in a thousand pieces of glass in a window—on a surface which is no surface, only a plane of direct light, broken, enriched, transformed by a singular interruption of glass and lead. A new phenomenon will not be understood by applying old laws. You cannot explain the weightlessness of a man in space by any positive reference to the laws of gravity, for he has moved out of the condition where these laws apply. Nevertheless new and utterly different conditions of space do not change the observable physiology of the man, only his activity in those conditions. If this analogy is broadly true, we see how the 'laws' or criteria by which we apprehend a work of creative transparency are intrinsically different from those traditionally applied to creative work in two or three dimensional solid surfaces.

It is possible to make a still finer point to our instrument of judgement. If you think of any device which is energized by the force of electricity, it is clear that you only perceive the effect of the force in the behaviour of the device—not the force itself. Should you, however, conduct an electric current into your body by touching a live wire you experience the force directly—as a physical shock. Applying this to our observation of art, we see that it is necessary for light waves to fall directly upon a painting, sculpture, or any other solid work before they can bounce indirectly to the eye, thus making an image on the retina of the effects of light—not light itself. On the other hand, the experience of looking at a window is to conduct into the eye the energy of light as a kind of shock on the retina.[1] This we can call the first great law of stained glass. The second derives from it—namely, that all transparent images conveyed by colour, line, or form, interrupting a source of light, become transformed and are perceived as a unique visual impact. As the astronaut, while apparently physically unchanged, behaves differently in a condition of weightlessness, so the body of artistic valuation, proportion, contrast, colour, tone, line, and so on, while still valid, appear to act differently in a condition of transparency. In short, we are going to look at windows, not as pictures, but as crystalline areas in buildings, which conjure with light itself to produce works of art of a unique kind.

---

[1] As support to the argument, there are two books which would be useful as marginal reading. *What is Light?* by A. C. S. van Heel and C. H. F. Velzel, World University Library, 1968, is a clear exposition of the phenomena for the layman, and *The Radiance at Chartres* by J. R. Johnson, Phaidon Press, 1964, is an examination of the transformed effect of light produced by the internal structure of the glass and complex colour combinations in the windows at Chartres.

Deerhurst, Priory church. 14th century. Detail from the West windows, South aisle, of donors, probably members of the de Hauteville family.

CHAPTER 2

The Framework

It must be supposed that we all have some memory of a church—in fact these words may have already called some image to mind, some witness that lingers at the fringe of memory, defying definition. Even if one's experience of a church is recent, it is likely to be vague in recollection (unless one is an architect or an expert in ecclesiastical matters) and this may be due to the special atmosphere engendered by a spiritually orientated building. As we tend to lower our voice in church, so we tend to lower our perceptions and come away with impressions of windows, for instance, blurred by sentiment or prejudice to the extent that we are quite unable to fix clearly in the mind how good or bad a window was in absolute artistic terms or even how the thing was made.

Those who have an interest in the arts above the average have a fairly accurate idea of how paint is applied to canvas or how a piece of sculpture is carved or modelled, but there is a deep ignorance about how stained glass is made. In Kenneth Clark's book *Civilization* it is interesting to note that, even with one of his scholarship and wide understanding, there is a certain coyness in his reference to the windows at Chartres. These windows, which he ranks so highly in the total achievement of the Middle Ages, have been covered by some mere twenty lines of text and much of that is taken up in a general comment on the difficulty of appreciating the iconography. Architects, art historians and critics, who should know better, often have only the most rudimentary notion of the technique of leaded windows or how stained glass is best exploited in buildings. It is not our purpose to provide technical instruction, except in so far as it is a direct aid to appreciation. The reader may be referred to the author's previous book,[1] and to other books referred to in passing, for a full account of the processes involved. Nevertheless, the physical structure, the nature of glass, and other material problems are inextricably involved in the assessment of the degrees of artistry displayed in a window. It will be continually urged, as we proceed, that there is an intrinsic quality in the very material of glass, quite

[1] See Lawrence Lee, *Stained Glass*. Oxford Paperbacks Handbooks for Artists, O.U.P., 1967.

Bourges Cathedral. apart from what is done to it or what it is made to express, and I can think of no better way of understanding the nature of this than by a visit to a glass works. To see the changing beauty of the glowing liquid from the white-hot glory of the crucible to the gradual appearance of its inbred colour as the glow dies, is to experience in miniature something as primeval as the origins of our own earth.

Long Melford, Suffolk.   One of the disappointments experienced as we travel about looking for stained glass is to find how haphazard are the shapes and content of windows in a single church. All too rarely do we find places that are a superb architectural whole, like Bourges or Long Melford; very seldom indeed do we find them with their original glass more 13, 19 or less complete as at Chartres or Fairford. More often the village churches will be a hotchpotch of periods and style, with window openings of all kinds—single lancets, two-light, multi-light with tracery, wide, stanchioned classical windows with semi-circular heads, or modern, rectangular and metal-framed. The splendidly consistent Perpendicular church at Fairford in Gloucestershire with stonework and glass all of the same period must be set against, for instance, the remarkable church at Great Warley in Essex, built and furnished in the Art Nouveau style except for its windows, of which only one or two in the chancel are of the period. When it is realized that all but the more recent churches have undergone the vicissitudes of damage, neglect, restoration, or radical replanning, it is not surprising that the window structures and the glass they contain offer a bewildering variety of treatment. Add to this the doctrinal upheavals in religion that followed the Reformation, resulting in great fluctuations of opinion about what should be taken out of, or put into, the subject matter of windows, and it is not surprising that lack of cohesion is likely to be the rule. Worse still was the emergence of the individual donor more intent on leaving concrete proof of his

Fairford, Gloucestershire.

piety than of enriching the house of God for its own sake. The all-important matter of positioning stained glass memorials was now governed, not by their architectural or even spiritual fitness, but by their proximity to the benefactor's family pew. In practice, this means you are likely to find a Gothic Revival church at one time sustained by a rich patronage, fully glazed with imitation fourteenth-century glass ordered *en masse* from a church furnisher with less thought than would be given to the choice of wallpaper. At the other extreme, we are all familiar with the dull, red-brick building, once a daughter church in some older suburb, where the congregation, never well-off, worship in the sad amber light of windows glazed in 'cathedral rolled' and never look at the one stained glass window in the north aisle that somehow got put in as a memorial to a long forgotten worthy. High, Broad, and Evangelical practices and all manner of uncharitableness have wrought much havoc but they are an essential background to any study of the human causes behind the periods we usually lump together as 'decadent' in stained glass. In spite of all this we still have in England a great many churches of harmonious beauty, and much stained glass that merits patient travel and study.

With individual windows we are presented, first of all, with a fixed frame, a containment of stone, brick, or wood which existed before the fixing of the glass and lead panels and which arbitrarily imposes its sanctions regardless of the artist's wishes in the matter. Secondly, and as a consequence of this, we are faced with largely unalterable factors of light, height, and extraneous clutter. A window may be partially obscured by a tree or a building darkening and perhaps casting awkward shadows across its surfaces; it may be very high up in a clerestory and difficult to see in a narrow nave, or hidden away behind the organ; or it may have part of its lower half cut off by a monstrosity of a reredos installed with equal disregard for cost and architecture. The 'picture' we have to study is, therefore, quite unlike the single painting in a suitable frame, nicely hung and lit and surveyed (with helpful catalogue notes) from the comfort of a seat in an art gallery. Rather it is seen as an area of qualified light in a solid wall, its 'canvas' broken into one or more vertical divisions (mullions) and divided horizontally by numerous saddle bars, while above its springing line what is left of its light is condensed into trefoils, quatrefoils, cinqfoils, or other shapes collectively described as tracery.

Fairford. One of the Gospel story windows which form part of a unique exposition of the 'Poor man's bible' remaining more or less complete. 16th century.

Great Malvern,
Worcestershire, East
window: exterior
(above), and interior.

Looking up at the outside of the great east window at Malvern Priory one has the impression of wide stone mullions holding an enormous iron grill of interlocking stanchions and horizontal bars and relatively small areas of uncluttered glass. Yet, such is the power of light, the same window seen from the nave inside appears light and open, its imagery floating in a silvery light, apparently without support. This phenomenon is known as 'halation' or the spreading of light round the solid interruptions. It makes the optical size of the window or its parts appear more extensive than the actual dimensions of the opening. The heaviness of stonework or of the ironwork disappears in this condition of light, and many observers have admired a window without even noticing the existence of these intrusions. The power of light expanding beyond solids is something known to most people in one form or another, but it is not often appreciated that in coloured glass light appears to expand or 'gather' more with one colour than another. We shall have more to say on this in Chapter 7 where we shall also discuss other optical peculiarities, but for the moment enough has been said to make it clear that, before purely artistic evaluations are made, these simple, physical conditions must be reckoned with. When they have been fully understood and brought into the general harmony we have the essential ground from which great work can spring. Bad windows may be technically perfect but insensitive to light, either killing it or admitting it without control. This is often the case with stereotyped church furnishers' windows. Conversely, a highly original window from the hand of a real artist may be diminished by bad leading or ill considered placing of saddle bars or even by failure to fit properly, resulting in botched up cementing into the stonework. There have been cases of eventual loss of drawing when unsuitable pigments, badly fired, succumb to the thermal shocks of heat and cold and flake off.

These, then, are the conditions of a glazed opening, and the astonishing range of expression by individual artists within these disciplines is one of the more pleasurable surprises we shall experience.

In a work on the aesthetics of any major art it is normal to assume that the reader is familiar with the names and reputations of many of the artists concerned in its development. The names of Michelangelo and Rubens may summon up not only mental pictures of their works, but also a variety of impressions of the artists themselves as people. In fact, we tend sometimes to think of them as colourful individuals about whom has gathered that accretion of fact and legend which goes to make up the romantic tradition of the great artist; only as an afterthought do we recall one of their paintings or sculptures. Though this popular notion of artists and their work is superficial and often misinformed, at least it gives a writer some commonly understood scaffolding on which to develop his thesis. We may read of Giotto, the impact he had on his contemporaries and the influence on artists that followed, and we recognize his style or 'handwriting' when we see his work. We say 'Ah, here is a Giotto' or, if uncertain, at least someone of his period or tradition. The hub of art was centred for so long in Italy, that we are all familiar with the names of Italian artists from quite early times; the artists of Reformation Germany and the Low Countries come later, and not till the eighteenth century can we actually bring to mind a few names of English painters.

The cult of the artist's 'name' is, however, very recent in the time-span of creative man. Even in Italy documented artists are rare before Cimabue; we should find difficulty in putting names to such notable works as the Ravenna mosaics or to that little masterpiece called the Wilton Diptych. In general terms, the great mass of art before the Quattrocento tends to be anonymous. The few names unearthed by archaeologists from these early days are significant only to art historians. In what are usually described as the minor arts, the works of craft like jewellery, pottery, and so on, names of craftsmen are not commonly known until about the sixteenth century. Innumerable European artists and craftsmen of all centuries are unnamed and if to them we add all those creative workers of all times, all places, and all works which we admire in our museums and historic sites, it begins to look as if anonymous art is far more common than 'named' art. Stained glass, whether you call it a major or a

Canterbury Cathedral, West window, head of king. 15th century.

minor art, is to this day often the production of virtually unnamed artists. Exceptions to this will be noted when we discuss particular examples—mostly of the nineteenth and twentieth centuries. But we must face the problem that we have to explain some fairly noble works of man without the faintest idea of who produced them. Even if we did, it is doubtful if their names would conjure up persons of such solid character or eccentricity as Turner or Whistler.

The little we know of successful glaziers in history can soon be told. We could expand the matter with reference to a great many records, accompanied by impressive textual analysis, or cloak our uncertainties with the annotations of interminable sources. This is not the purpose of this book. There are fascinating glimpses which could be pursued. I particularly like the reference to a tombstone of Roman times discovered at Lyon, commemorating an 'artist in glass of African nationality and a citizen of Carthage';[1] or the grant of a lifeholding of a house and an acre of vineyard to Fulk, eleventh-century painter-glazier, in return for working throughout his life on windows for the Abbot Girard's abbey; and the grant of a prebendaryship to glaziers by the Bishop of Auxerre between 1052 and 1070.[2]

I suppose the least we can say of such men, and those that followed is that they may have been in the same class, in terms of reputation, as are those now widely recognized by art historians and antique dealers as masters—Tompion the clockmaker, Paul de Lamerie the silversmith, or Chippendale the chairmaker. In any event, I am certain it is inaccurate to think of them as simple mechanicals like Bottom the weaver, Snug the joiner, or Quince the carpenter. If stained glass was a commodity which could be privately collected (very small pieces do sometimes appear on the art market) the best would be as highly valued as the works of those other masters. Think what a price the Five Sisters from York Minster ('artist unknown', possibly York School, c. 1400) would fetch at auction at Sothebys! But the multi-millionaire who bought them would have a problem; unless he built a private chapel at least seventy feet high there would be no way of enjoying them. As art investment windows are not very practical. We are back again in the condition of architecture and its attendant non-detachable art. Frescoes are likewise

[1] Gordon Childe, *What Happened in History*. Penguin Books, 1942, p. 274.
[2] Maurice Drake, *A History of English Glass Painting*. Werner Laurie, 1912.

placed in relation to the wall, but their painters, at least in the centuries before the Renaissance, have stood out so that great names like Cimabue, Giotto, or Fra Angelico are accorded respect as authentic artists equal to Raphael, Rembrandt, or Gainsborough.

This is not the case with glaziers, and two main factors seem to me to account for their twilight reputations. The first is a material one. From prehistoric paintings in caves to the latest abstract painting acquired by the Tate Gallery or Metropolitan Museum of New York, the pigments used for drawing or colouring as well as the surfaces to which they were applied are not the thing we immediately 'see'. Though we know that the rock face or the rough unprimed canvas does impart some special texture to the work, we are mainly held by the images the artist has created—be they charging bison or abstract areas of colour. In sculpture it is much the same, although the special qualities of wood, stone, or metal have perhaps more to say, it is still usually secondary to the representation of a figure or other objects. It is not my thesis to argue about the influence of materials and technique on the full and final appreciation of the fine arts; for me they are not in question. If, however, we think of other materials— textiles, ceramics, precious metals, and stones and glass—we are conscious of the material taking over, by virtue of its intrinsic quality, from the images or subjects printed, woven, hammered, or carved on or into them. These we call 'creative' crafts. Some things usually classified in this category such as mosaic, tapestry, and stained glass don't quite fit. Often monumental in size and with the same ability to present flat, two-dimensional pictures as painting, they have called for much the same basic skills. But, and this is the crucial point, it is only when works in these mediums are openly expressing the materials of which they are made—made, not painted—that they are truly great. A full-sized painted copy of the Ravenna mosaics stuck up on the walls of San Vitale would give itself away immediately. What painter would consider it worth while to copy a tapestry which conveyed every tone and texture of the interlocking threads or, *reductio ad absurdum*, who would think of placing a painted imitation coloured window over an existing one—thereby blocking the very element by which we see it? So, pre-eminently in glass, the medium is the message. The artist who tries to express his ideas in glass is at once humbled by its intractability and outshone by its gift of light.

The second factor is equally important but harder to describe.

It is to do with one of those limitations mentioned earlier, the restriction of the art almost wholly to one religion and in one relatively small part of the world, a part which did not come within the orbit of that growth of art consciousness we now associate with the fine arts. Though we may find the trades of painters, sculptors, weavers, metal-workers, and potters in almost any part of the inhabited world, the trade of glaziers, as a skill with artistic possibilities, begins to diminish the further we move outward from the northern hemisphere and in the hotter and remoter lands glazing is little more than a strictly utilitarian job. It would seem that windows which are used to create spiritually significant atmospheres of light, colour, and design tend to be at their best in those parts of the globe which have a temperate climate, with its associated preponderance of dull days. Historically this has inclined buildings less to inviting the play of strong sunshine on external architectural forms than to encouraging, by the use of large windows, whatever light is available to illuminate the internal structure. The demand for large windows in northern European churches required from the glazier a response which, because the demand was in a Christian context, was necessarily conditioned by religion. His identity became to some extent embedded in an intention that was outside himself and infinitely larger than any notion he may have had of his own importance.

In addition to this was the fact already mentioned of the intrinsic beauty and power of the glass, which, by an odd paradox often seduce the spectator from admiration of the artist to a fascination with his material. It could be said that the greater the skill in the creative use of light passing through glass the less obvious is the hand that created it; the greater the authentically spiritual effect, the less the concern with the labour which achieved it. The fact that some entrancing details in painted glass are often found in high traceries where only binoculars can bring them to a size sufficient for full appreciation is surely a sign that the artist knew himself to be engaged on work whose sanction was more than public approbation. I think we may say that the eye of his judge was set at some higher and remoter point than the congregation on the floor of the nave. Be that as it may, the modern device of the telephoto lens has brought down some of these delightful details into our focus and when, all too rarely, we see them on the television screen we recognize with sudden pleasure the hand of an artist, authentic but anonymous.

The modern stained glass artist is often thought of as a nice religious sort of chap, who because he is associated with church art, much of which is bad, is not much of an artist. The robust oaths and elegant blasphemies that can usually be heard in stained glass studios should remind us that he is not necessarily religious (in a narrow sense) and rarely an orthodox Christian; the assessment of his place in the world of art is what this book is about and our hope is that some sort of balanced judgement can be made by the time it is finished. The medieval glazier suffered no such disadvantage. All art was, in one degree or another, religious and he could work with unselfconscious ease—oaths and blasphemies included. With the mastery of his 'mystery' he would become aware of the universal Church, rich in imagery and symbolism; he would have a fairly assured demand for his work, sometimes bringing opportunities for travel to distant cathedrals or abbeys, often with the offer of better pay. A master like John Thornton, having established a reputation among the flourishing school of glaziers in Coventry, could be asked to take on the glazing of the great East window in York Minster. Five years later he would be made a Freeman of the City, and, a man of some substance now, would own property in York and Coventry. These men were severely practical. They had contracts with the Dean and Chapter for definite terms of employment and rates of pay.

Philip Nelson, in a chapter on medieval glaziers notes that

in 1351 ... the sum of £145 was expended on glass for the windows of St. Stephen's Chapel at Westminster. 'Those who work on the drawing of images, draw and paint on white tables, several drawings for windows' were six in all, viz. Master John de Chester, John Athelard, John de Lincoln, Simon de Lynne, John Lenton and Hugh de Lichesfield, all of whom are termed master glaziers and all of whom received 1s. per diem, the first occasionally being paid 7s. per week.[1]

Glass had to be bought—the whites mainly locally in England and the colours mostly from Flanders; what was available had to be taken and, because of costs and difficulty of transport, the glaziers used a strictly limited palette. They did not work in monkish isolation with the finest material sent straight from God to the accompaniment of heavenly choirs. Theirs was the clatter and dirt of the glazier's shop with a hundred day-to-day practical problems to be sorted out,

York Minster, East window. Made by John Thornton between 1405 and 1408. For size alone it is one of the most remarkable windows in the world.

[1] Philip Nelson, *Ancient Painted Glass in England*. Methuen, 1913, p. 39.

assistants to direct, and difficult churchmen to deal with. They were, into the bargain, taxed on their stock of glass. How or where such artists had learnt their drawing and design is not certain, but the application to the materials of glass, glass paint, stain, and lead is complete; the idea of drawing and painting as an isolated academic exercise would be quite foreign to them. When the artist painted a head, with the rough drawing on the whitened bench as a guide, he would proceed to draw directly onto the glass with a brush loaded with pigment like wet mud. The surface of the greenish white glass, already cut to an approximate shape, was slippery, offering no 'bite'. The painter had to apply his whole experience of how things would 'read' against the light, right down to the ultimate hairline point of his brush and then, like the oriental calligrapher, commit himself to a stroke without hesitation or second thought.

29 The resultant drawing was often superb in its economy, control, and expressiveness and, since the artist was not just decorating a surface but conveying a representation of a man or woman, he would, at his best, suggest subtlety of emotion or character within the very fine limits of an instinctive synthesis of the interaction of direct light on line and tone. In these circumstances a great draughtsman like Michelangelo would be utterly at sea.

Later, when glass painters began to imitate High Renaissance painting on glass it could be said that the art of glass painting began to decline. This judgement may sound a little doctrinaire. Undoubtedly from the start Italian glass in particular showed a special interest in, and aptitude for, the representation of natural appearance. This is not surprising, following as it did the revival of the depiction of volume and depth as well as the more naturalistic style inaugurated by Giotto —in the circumstances an inevitable development and not necessarily to be deplored if one appreciates the great beauty of the thirteenth- and early fourteenth-century windows at Assisi, Ravenna, Bologna, and Siena. However, one has only to see the later windows designed

30 by Ghirlandaio and Perugino (to name only two established painters employed to design windows) to become aware of the trend of the painter's mind, obsessed with human appearance, gradually eroding the Gothic designers' concept of significant action within a relatively flat abstraction of shapes and colours.

I have to ask the questions: was the painters' mastery of composition in three-dimensional space inimical to that heraldic display of subject

Detail of painted head from Westminster Abbey. 15th century. Now in the Victoria and Albert Museum.

Florence, Santo Spirito, design after Perugino. 15th century. Photo Alinari.

which I believe to be essential to the medium of glass? Should a striving after a purely local emotion expressed through solid figures with up-turned, foreshortened faces have overruled the Gothic designers' instinctive reticence in demonstrating purely ephemeral attitudes? Was it a dereliction of the timeless quality of monumental art to make heavy groups of figures and level ranks of faces on a flat earth which recedes to a natural horizon and an atmospheric sky— abandoning the medieval designers' itemization of their story over an uptilted earth and a flat unearthly firmament? Here, for the moment, I must rest my case and return to the anonymous austerity of northern Europe.

The unique contribution made by English Medieval glaziers is now beginning to be appreciated, if only by the negative process of discovering how much of it is in urgent need of restoration and conservation. It is impossible to assess how many splendid windows have been lost by wilful damage, neglect, or simple ignorance of the fragility of works of art which, had they not been doing the work of keeping out the weather, would have survived undamaged in museums. As I have said before in this connection:

Unlike dense materials, glass is something we look through not at and, so long as it appears to hang together in its pervious leads, bewitched by the beauties of the eroded colours and scavenged paintwork, we do not question its survival. Yet by its own unstable nature, assisted by the weathering of the world's winds and rains, glass is trying to return to that unclear silica from which it came.[1]

So, while they are still with us, may we take pleasure in the windows that remain and honour the men who made them: Edward, appointed master glazier to Henry III and perhaps the first to whom we can put a name; those who glazed Becket's Crown at Canterbury or those responsible for the Jesse Tree at York Minster, a fragment of which still remains; or Thomas the glazier, employed by William of Wykeham to make the windows of Winchester College Chapel, and John Prudde, contracted for the windows of the Beauchamp Chapel at Warwick; or the Pety family, glaziers to York Minster from 1447–1578; and many more of whom space does not allow a mention.

But, named or unnamed, the medieval glazier by sheer cunning and skill did often produce little masterpieces of glass and paint which have never had their full acknowledgement. This chapter, then, is dedicated to the unknown glazier and the missing names on a roll of honour of art; to men who may have been as honoured among citizens as Cimabue, as outrageous as Benvenuto Cellini or as quiet and workmanlike as George Stubbs—to men whose work is their only memorial.

Winchester College chapel. Detail from restored East window. Thomas the Glazier. 14th century.

[1] Leaflet, 'Care of Historic Glass'. Council for Places of Worship.

Our way is now, I hope, reasonably clear to a place where we can talk about finding and seeing windows. Observation in the field is most rewarding when a student not only has a very clear idea of what he is looking for, but also the equipment necessary to find it: an examination of a garden pool for aquatic life is one thing, but an exploration of the upper Amazon quite another. Finding worthwhile windows takes one outside the normal concentration of art which civilized communities gather into art galleries and museums. It requires a good deal of zig-zagging travel, and even when a site is reached the observer may have to sort out which are good windows from a number of indifferent or bad ones. Architecture shares this difficulty. Both tend to have very important modern examples tucked away in places far off the main routes, places such as Ronchamp, 41, 50, 42, 48 Assy, Vence, Yvetot, Audincourt in France; Tudeley, Oundle, 71 Winchelsea, Wellingborough in England; Saarbrücken, Cologne, title page Aachen in Germany; or Woonsocket and Stamford in the United States. This is to name entirely at random a few villages, towns, or cities where important modern windows can be seen; if we are also looking for historic glass we would have to stop at every old-looking church in sight in case some interesting glass was still to be seen. When I spoke of a 'field' study it was intended as a fairly accurate metaphor.

The problem this presents is—how shall we know what to look for? Windows, even by fairly well-known artists, are scarcely ever labelled, some are signed with a cipher, few are mentioned in the church guide-book. This still leaves out those windows that are profitable to study but for which there is no clue to authorship (except to experts) nor any catalogue of dates.

Another of the disadvantages from which stained glass suffers is the rich field it offers to antiquarians. They are quite naturally and properly attracted to the fragmentary survivals, indirect documentation, and fascinating historical by-ways the subject opens up to the purely detective mind. It is necessary to elaborate, as some people have been put off by this all too evident approach in so many books on historical glass. For example:

Wyeman, in his attempt to date the window, was troubled by the apparel of the cardinal in panel VI of the lower row. 'He is wearing a red cloak as well as a red hat, and if the generally accepted statement that a cardinal did not wear a red robe until 1464 is correct, the window cannot have been of an earlier date.'

Actually the rules were laid down in Rome in 1310, although in foreign countries these rules do not seem to have been strictly observed, *particularly by artists* [my italics]. As right up to the middle of the fifteenth century glass painters continued to represent cardinals in robes of all colours, it is clear that nothing as to date can be deduced from the red robe in the Palmers' window. For example, there are portraits of Cardinal Peter of Luxemburg. . . .[1]

This quotation is typical of the careful archaeological-detective approach. It is not the purpose of such writers to give help to the willing but uninstructed eyes of the reader, but rather to supply a pinch of snuff to the collector's nose. Contrast with this:

. . . its windows were never so brilliant as on days when the sun scarcely shone, so that if it was dull outside you might be certain of fine weather in church. One of these was filled . . . by a solitary figure, like a king on a playing card, who lived up there beneath his canopy of stone, between earth and heaven. . . . And all of them were so old that you could see, here and there, their silvery antiquity sparkling with the dust of centuries and showing in its thread-bare brilliance the very cords of their lovely tapestry of glass.[2]

Proust makes me want to seek out this church and see the king for myself, and I shall not bother with dating his crown on stylistic grounds or his robe on protocols laid down at arbitrary dates in history.

It brings us once more into the open air of visual adventure and to the place where discoveries are made before rules; and though we may refer of necessity to rules, systems, conventions, and other devices of the mind's pattern-making, it is to this place of free understanding that we must eventually return. It could indeed be argued that, given reasonable knowledge of art history and an intelligent and flexible approach to aesthetics, we should be able to sort things out for ourselves. In my experience this does not always happen. People with all these qualifications still tend to come back and ask questions. Are the windows in St. Patrick's Cathedral, New

[1] E. W. Ganderton and Jean Lafond, *Ludlow Stained and Painted Glass*. Friends of the Church of St. Lawrence Ludlow, 1961.

[2] Marcel Proust, *Du Côté de chez Swann*. Translated by C. K. Scott Moncrieff.

York, really old or are they copies of European cathedral windows? Who did the nave windows in Coventry Cathedral? Why does the colour in some Swiss domestic glass appear to be painted on the glass rather than leaded up as separate pieces of colour?

The canon of good stained glass has been well drafted in the past but the usual clauses in this canon often take a great deal for granted. By any legalistic interpretations of these 'constitutions', very many of the types of windows shown in the illustrations to this book as, for one reason or another, mediocre, stereotyped, or fraudulent, might just get by as 'good'. And because this canon is not as familiar as the old laws of the fine arts by reason of the unique technical or environmental factors, a number of experimental and empirical judgements will have to be made to get things arranged in reasonable order in our minds. We shall have to take it for granted that in looking at anything that is aesthetically significant to ourselves, we are bound to be affected by our predispositions, prejudices, and all those observed precedents in other visual arts that make up that instinctive attraction, repulsion, or indifference to what we see.

Elements of these predispositions are traceable in the foregoing chapters. They are recognized as (1) the usually confused condition of the art, (2) the curious ignorance of the technical aspects of the craft, (3) the generally anonymous state of the artists employed in its making, and (4) the inevitable atmosphere of religion and antiquarianism. All these can create a kind of front in the mind which may frustrate the ultimate pleasure we all seek in our appreciation of the arts.

But if we forget all art history and criticism, all those visual associations of sophisticated art culture our brains have inherited, I think we have to accept that some signals from eye to cortex, cortex to interpretation are the same, in all human beings. The formation of abstract vocal symbols (or words) is unique to the human consciousness and leads to grammar and signals of speech. There is a corresponding grammar or arrangement of visual apprehension, though in its more highly developed form it leaves the workaday world of accepted signals having more or less equal values for all of us, and becomes remote, impossible to define, and in the last resort intuitive. In verbal arrangement the same must be said of poetry.

I think it is important to say this in the context of *all* our visual experiences, even those which we may think to be utterly personal,

Penshurst, Kent. The Becket window (detail). Lawrence Lee. Note the use of heraldic idiom in the semi-abstraction of the figures.

even secret to ourselves alone. For what is the use of art if it is not to reach out by externalizing those very secrets to a correspondence in our fellow men? Of what purpose was Bonnard's struggle to a final synthesis of his vision about a woman lying in a bath—iridescence of tiles above her reflecting from the sunny room beyond—if it was not an intense experience to which, though he alone could externalize it, we can all react with breathless delight—as though we too had been there all the time. The *Nu dans la baignoire* hidden from me for so many years, the exquisite tracery of light hidden for centuries high up in the cathedral clerestory and now revealed to me by the telephoto lens—whether you call these things done for God or unconsciously for some total consciousness, these individual images must become visible to other individuals if they are to complete their incarnation. As Harold Osborne says,[1] the art of appreciation is a skill and the 'becoming visible' involves the artist's skill and the observer's skill in an interplay of foresights, insights, bafflements, and resolution unique to the reflecting creature called man.

Imagine, if you will, that you could set a guard over that first area

Nu dans la baignoire.
Bonnard.

[1] *The Art of Appreciation.* O.U.P., 1970.

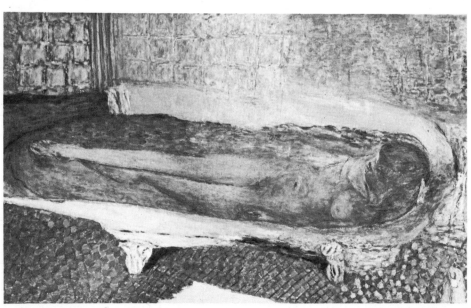

of the visual cortex so that the image received from the eye is momentarily protected from all associations not apposite to the immediacy of the thing seen, then you would be in that first, but essential, state of vision necessary to the making and seeing of art. You may say this is hackneyed stuff—the child's vision, the poet's vision, Blake and all the world in a grain of sand—and so it is. But it needs to be said with special emphasis in relation to looking at stained glass. If it were not so, I would not have felt compelled to write this chapter. There are such deep and often unconscious hindrances to the clear appraisal of windows reported by all the stained glass artists I have ever met that I cannot put aside my own experience as accidental. These hindrances can be summarized under three headings: (1) the hindrance of association with simple craft, (2) the hindrance of association with church art, and (3) the hindrance of association with picture making. From the first springs the reverence for mere craft, for beautiful workmanship and beautiful materials, leading to admiration for mere skill and such things as 'the marvellous colours of the glass'—or there is the opposite attitude of some *avant garde* artists who, with puritan zeal, reject the seduction of light and colour which is proper to the medium. From the second comes a host of difficulties stemming from quite fundamental misconceptions about religion, leading to a false respect based on a false sentiment or a false condemnation based on false premises. The third hindrance is the commonest form of misunderstanding and leads to irrelevant admiration of all naturalistic effects simply because they are culled forth from improbable materials like glass and lead; or for those taking the opposite critical position—the rejection of any representation in a 'decorative craft'—the unequivocal condemnation of anything that is not flat, archaic in design, or devoid of all subject-matter.

A mixture of these hindrances, with sometimes more of one ingredient than another, in general leads to the two positions we may call left or right, modern or traditional. Those with the attitude on the right of centre tend to believe in 'traditional' church art, handed down from a Gothic Sinai and never to be questioned, while those to the left of centre will tend to believe only in highly personal 'modern' experiments in glass, each work of art its own Sinai and not to be questioned; the one is passive, generally orthodox Christian, the other active and often anti-clerical. This brusque type-cast is obviously unfair and I plead avoidance of the symmetrical trap by the use of the word 'tend'.

Among sincere church-goers there are many who have a finely cultured intelligence in matters of art and are fully alive to the best in historical and contemporary glass. Conversely, you may find among some intellectuals an anti-clericalism so subjective that they are quite unable to make fair critical appreciation of religious art—particularly post-Reformation work—though they must of necessity take note of religious works by renowned masters such as Matisse, Léger, and Sutherland. Unquestioned subjectivism is always bad, but in the public arts it is disastrous. One man's prejudice either for 'traditional art' or 'modern art', though quite proper to the decoration of his own home, should not impose itself on the selection of work for a large audience. This is no argument for 'committee' art, which so often ends up with the lowest agreed solution rather than the highest. It is an argument for the things that this series of books is all about. It does not matter if the artists selected for making paintings, sculptures, or windows for public buildings are chosen by one man or twenty, if that one man or those twenty are dedicated to a full and deep appreciation of the arts. The enlightened patron or the enlightened corporation is all one can ask and hope for.

In those periods when glass and masonry were more or less harmonious in conception and execution, there was sufficient common ground between the people and the artist to ensure that windows expressed a common, implicit intention, and sometimes this could lift it to a plane, not perhaps expected but ultimately understood by the onlookers. The artists' private images were not different in kind but only in the degree of the physical realization in design and colour. The French medieval peasant might stand amazed at the glories of colour that were going up in his new Cathedral of Our Lady at Chartres, but the amazement was at the skill, splendour, and sheer monumentality—not at the subject matter (or images) with which he was already familiar. In a sense his own mental images, nurtured by the church liturgy were only made flesh by the artist: the windows enclosed his spiritual home and peopled the light with potent extensions of his own mythology. His appreciation had, therefore, an immediacy that comes from being visually literate—a quality still found among some cultures with common imagery but without formal (literary) education. Those who now stand and gaze

Hillingdon Hospital chapel, Middlesex. Glass appliqué by Jane Gray (detail). Though abstract, the concept begins with the idea of positive and negative forces, expressed, not only in colour, but in the opposing lines.

at the Chartres windows are still amazed and delighted but few can read the imagery. They may, of course, intuitively read the maternal tenderness of the Belle Verrière, for she spans all time and all cultures and speaks direct to the baffled heart of man. Paradoxically, the common view of the illiterate peasant having his religion explained in pictures is reversed; it is now the modern visitor, often visually illiterate, who needs to have the pictures explained by means of a booklet. A common criticism of the nave windows in the new cathedral at Coventry is just this—that they need a booklet to explain them. But if they had been composed of realistic illustrations of Old and New Testament subjects, they would still need explanation. The modern visitor must come at it the other way round. First, seduced by light, colour, and design, he must be led to look further through some primitive response between the eye and the ever-inquiring brain to a fuller appreciation of the subject matter. For it is certain that however abstract the first impression may be, the artist has always started with a subject—whether you call the 'subject' idea, image, inspiration, concept, or even divine influence.

54, 55

No creation can start in a vacuum—in fact no man's mind can ever be a vacuum, try as he may. And the common structure of the mind, in artist or spectator, is enough to begin with for the rewarding process of teasing out our bafflement with modern art. We do have

39

this common ground if for instance in circumstances where great noise is inappropriate we quite justifiably say that a piece of music is being played too loud; in similar circumstances we can say with equal assurance of a window having violent colour that it, too, is strident or 'noisy'. When dealing with colour I shall extend the musical analogy, but for the moment it is interesting to consider how often the spectator of windows might be called a listener. The readiness of the layman seeking progress in the appreciation of music to allow the ear to evaluate more and more precisely the relationships of sound vibrations as they strike the eardrum is not unlike that to which the serious spectator of windows commits himself—in his case the evaluation of direct light vibrations striking the retina.

If on succeeding pages we talk of unendurable 'glare', may it not be the same as speaking of unendurable sound vibrations; if we talk of unsuitable violence of colour or scale, may it not be the same as speaking of unsuitable violence of pitch or volume. We must be agreed at least that the sound of 'Jail-house rock' would be unsuitable for the setting of the 'Magnificat'; we must be agreed that the 'Ride of the Valkyries' is unendurable as the music for a lullaby. Inappropriate treatments are blasphemous but they are also emotionally suicidal. I have an acquaintance, now elderly, who as a girl would burst into tears on looking at a particularly mawkish Victorian window representing Faith, Hope, and Charity, despite assurances that these ghastly virtues were not as grim as they were shown. The opposite is also true. The same lady told me that she recently saw a modern semi-abstract window and 'it gave her tingles of delight down her spine'. Though all our aesthetic appreciation is not so dramatic as this, it is clear in the final analysis that emotion is a dominant factor, coming sometimes early, sometimes later, in our fully rounded acceptance or rejection of a work of art.

When I first saw colour reproduction of the windows of Matisse for Notre-Dame du Rosaire, Vence, a sense of uncertainty—not affront—at their stark simplicity was uppermost. Now that I can appreciate the total environment in which they are set and which they to a large extent create, I am no longer unsure but drawn into the certainty of inevitability. Part of this conversion from a state of question to one of acceptance is the recognition of the fact that apparent simplicity is an illusion. Like most great acts of creation, it is a statement of imperative wholeness derived from a complexity

Vence, Chapel of the Rosary. Matisse.

so subtle that it is only fathomed by working down from the flat appearance of the glass to the mind that evolved it in this particular way. This is the vital work of the spectator and it is a work that the artist must allow him or they are each diminished. The more I appreciate the subtlety of the simplicity, the more I see how beautifully complexities of light, colour, and shape have been brought to a point where the artist and myself float, as it were, in a state of happy assurance with each other. This state is rather rare and its absence is not necessarily evidence of lack of creativeness in the artist or failure to appreciate in the spectator. There is enjoyment of art of many orders and intensities, and there are works which precipitate the rarer state only late in life, provided the mind has not been stopped at some gate of prejudice, marking a boundary which does not exist.

Another sort of work may cause a distressing involvement with the process of creation rather than the accomplished thing. The deceptive simplicity—the absence of clues to the complexity of the

41

artists thought—involves us in a disturbing argument with the artist, and this in the case of windows, which are fixtures, is liable to go on for a long time—over many generations in fact. In the church at Tudeley, Kent, there is a window by Marc Chagall which I have had the opportunity of studying closely. I still find it uncomfortable in the sense in which I have just spoken. The dialogue is incomplete—either through some lack in me or (though I resist this idea most strongly) through some lack in the artist. Glass is a hard taskmaster, reaping where it has not sown, and even a renowned master in paint, his dreams floating unencumbered on the canvas, may find himself in trouble when brought up against the sharp edge of glass. To merge is impossible. Ultimately the glass must stop: the large plain area of background to the essential image, in a painting requiring no punctuation, must now be broken with arbitrary veins of lead; a gentle movement of tone and colour, needing only the slightest linear accent, is lost against the black ditch that must, of practical necessity, break its flow. This is a problem peculiar to stained glass, and it is expounded in Chapter 5 when we deal with the question of surface continuity in the structure of a window. But we have to ask ourselves if Matisse's disciplined simplicity is unconsciously in line with the principles of glazing, while Chagall's apparently more conscious efforts are not. The antithesis implicit in this question may be false. I only offer it as an example of the kind of inquiry that must arise if we are to give works by such masters the serious attention they deserve not merely as just another 'painting' which happens to be in glass, but as a new kind of creation to which the medium of glass has brought an unfamiliar light, structure, and, if you will, 'sound'.

You and I, as spectators—partakers rather—of the work of the artist, must determine to know by looking, putting aside all purely verbal or literary formulas and the prejudice that so easily besets us, till we come to the place beyond superficial blandishments, beyond distaste even, to the just point of meeting—or departure.

Tudeley, Kent. Memorial to a drowned girl. Chagall.

The first impact of a window, whether the spectator is aware of it or not, is its scale. By scale I mean not only its actual dimensions but also the fundamental impression of size and proportion in all the elements of pattern, figures, imagery, and even colour, that are presented to the spectator in relation to a particular architectural setting. Scale in this all-embracing sense really defies definition. Not being an architect or a mathematician, I can only discuss it as it seems to me, trying to evoke in the reader a response to general laws; to make more explicit some of the implicit reactions we have to the size of things—how the bigness or smallness of one thing in relation to another conveys a sense of assurance or discomfort by its rightness or wrongness.

Stained glass is sometimes called a 'monumental' craft because of its association with large or monumental buildings (for a cathedral might be called a monument). With all large buildings devoted to a cult it is necessary to bear two points in mind. First, that they assert their authority by actual size. The new Coventry Cathedral is small in contrast to many of its European precursors, but it had to be about 100 feet high and proportionately extensive in length or it might have been seen as no more than a large parish church. The second point, for most cults, complements the first. Having asserted its size the building must also establish its humanity; it must appear to relate to the human beings it is supposed to serve by a series of modulations or intervals in the structure, proportioned in such a way as to assure us of grandeur without pomposity, authority without despotism, and spirituality without terror.

These psychological reactions are important and are used by different cultures in different ways. Adolf Hitler's dream of a new Berlin conceived early in his rise to power, expressed his contempt for his fellow men by its emphasis on enormous size. His *Prachtstrasse* was planned to have an avenue 400 feet wide and the new Führerpalast to be 20 times larger than the old Chancellory, while his *Kuppelhalle* (or secular cathedral) would have contained St. Peter's seven times over as Arnold Speer, Hitler's architect, pointed out. The inhumanity of this project is obvious. Less obvious is the effect of size uncon-

44

sciously developed by buildings serving modern industry. The enormous cooling towers associated with power stations are interesting in this context. Standing like great concrete vases in the landscape, their scale, though felt to be huge, lacks recognizable module or unit of construction, such as the bricks of the conventional factory chimney, and the uncomfortable ambiguity is only resolved by seeing them in relation to some traditional structure such as the local parish church—at one time the highest building in the countryside.[1]

The same reactions continue to operate in our assessment of smaller and more complex intervals in the details of a building or —in our case—in the details of a window. Artists have usually understood how to exploit them in practical ways. For instance, most of us, unpractised in gauging size, will tend to underestimate the height or parts of the height of a distant object. It is interesting to test this in judging the size of a man seen at some distance and above ground level—say, standing on the cill of a clerestory window in a large church or cathedral. We shall almost always overestimate; we find it difficult to believe how small a man would look at such a distance. Remembering this, it is obvious that when figures were used in high windows or carved over the great portals of a cathedral, they would have to be larger than life size. Depending on height, figures would be made a good deal larger than life but the artists of the Middle Ages seemed to stop short of anything approaching the colossal. Their figures would suggest great majesty but a majesty still related to man. Perhaps this was an especially Christian intuition

47

[1] The subject of scale has been dealt with more fully and expertly in Sinclair Gauldie's book on *Architecture* in the same series as the present book.

Sperrybridge cooling towers: note nearby parish church.

Wells Cathedral, clerestory light, showing use of base, figure, and canopy. 14th century.

stemming from the central doctrine of the Incarnation—God made man—and avoiding the final presumption, man made God. Only in the great pantocrators of the Italian Romanesque mosaics do we find really enormous representations, and these are seen from the waist up in the curved domes of the dark apse.

An opposite manipulation of the size of the human figure was employed in windows which were nearer to eye level. In this case actual life size was generally avoided in favour of a smaller scale. A height of about 4 feet 10 inches is common. For some reason the dimension of a figure occupying approximately one half of the total height of the light and placed a little below half-way up, leaving the remainder as base and canopy, works very satisfactorily. This is, after all, how one normally prefers to see a figure in a landscape— with a certain amount of ground (or base) to stand on and a fair amount of sky (or canopy) above in which to move. These proportions can still apply even in modern abstract work where the main mass of interest, or image, can act as the figure, supported by a lower and an upper interest roughly analogous to base and canopy.

A discussion of traditional applications of scale and proportion to figures and other subject matter, if applied only to historical stained glass up to about the mid nineteenth century, would be academic— like discussing the application of the Ten Commandments, never questioning the immutable laws they were assumed to embody. Now, however, in common with almost all aspects of man's activities, immutable law is in question. A manifestation of this 'disobedience' is seen in the greatly increased size of figures or images in some modern art. It is not merely a question of bigness (the Colossus at Rhodes and the heads of American presidents carved on Mt. Rushmore are freaks) but of *relative* bigness. In the East window of Eton College Chapel by Evie Hone, the figures in the lower range of lights are standing on the cills and their heads are almost touching the cusping at the top. The medieval proportions of base, figure, canopy have gone as they have in the remainder of the subject matter in the upper lights. It could be argued that, set in the delicate mullions and tracery of a typical Perpendicular window, this scale of figures and other subject matter does a disservice to the finely conceived masonry. One senses that the artist did not very much care about the architecture, being more concerned with a powerful personal expression of an idea. The point has been made by an admirer of Evie Hone's

46

Eton College chapel.
Evie Hone. Figure to
scale shown alongside.

undoubted talents in the little tribute published after her death:[1]
'Its first impact is almost too overwhelming. Her style with its
violence of colour was devised largely from the twelfth and thirteenth
centuries, and may be thought ill-suited to a fifteenth-century building.
The window makes the rest of the interior look flimsy.'

This comment brings us up against the difficulty (if such it is)

[1] *A Tribute to Evie Hone and Maimie Fellett,* edited by Stella N. Frost. Brown &
Nolan, 1957.

Oundle School chapel.
John Piper.

for modern artists who, not being working glaziers, are not in a position to have had the above 'rules' passed on to them, and who in any case would not necessarily regard them as relevant. Nevertheless, if an artist is required to design windows for installation in historical architectural settings which are themselves designed to

Icon, early 15th century.

take glass conceived in harmony with its frame, may we not place on him the onus of proving beyond doubt that his flouting of these proportions is justified? Within the figure itself it is quite possible to upset inherited predilection for what we regard as dignified or spiritual. There are cases of modern windows where the head of a figure is very large in proportion to the body and—like it or not— we are bound to be reminded of either children or dwarfs, with a consequent loss of dignity in the effect. The opposite reaction is experienced in looking at a good Russian icon. Here the heads, hands, and feet are small and the conventional highly wrought modelling of their flesh, contrasted with the flat patterned mass of the body, gives an impression of immense grace and spirituality. This slightly unearthly art—representing the 'wholly other' nature of God and His dealings with the world which is the special insight of the Orthodox Church—is perhaps too remote and uneasy for our restless materialistic Western minds. A more earthly but gently

49

beautiful insight into the otherness of pagan Arcady is seen in Botticelli's 'Primavera'. According to the classical canons of proportion for the human figure the head should be about one seventh of the total height. This would make these goddesses about nine feet tall; but we don't question them, for they are not of this world.

In looking at windows we shall be right to question both ourselves and the artist if we experience discomfort in these matters of scale. We may, by not appreciating the artist's real intention, be failing to understand just why he has adopted, for instance, large and disembodied hands or other symbolic objects, as does Léger in his Audincourt windows. On the other hand the artist could be wrong if he has ignored classical ideas of scale out of sheer wilfulness or self-assertion. In any case, we must not be misled by the mere slavish adherence to a set of rules followed so often by commercial windows that they have degenerated into a dead language: if this were the only test, they could be classed as good and those of Léger bad—which is nonsense.

Relieved of the necessity of a fixed, specially shaped and proportioned frame in which to design, any artist is free to create his own scale and you don't have to look at it if you don't want to. But once committed to the frame and the unavoidable public, the artist must accept responsibility to them both, while remaining true to his own convictions. This is a tight-rope situation which will arise in many forms as we proceed with discussions of colour, figures, and so on.

CHAPTER 6 Line

A leaded window is uniquely a matter of line. The word 'linear' is commonly used in the analysis of almost all arts, even non-visual ones such as music and poetry. But a window (unless it is plate glass) simply would not stand up without lines—black lines of lead or saddle bars and mullion—and hence the linear content is something which the artist has to come to terms with as a matter of necessity. The virtues arising from this necessity go without question in all the early glass. The later decadence could be explained, rather over-simply, by saying that there was an increasing tendency to make a vice of necessity and we could go on to say that the resurgence of the art in modern times is expressed in the rediscovery of the rightness of the earlier linear principles. The Jesse Tree window, the choir windows at Aachen, the East window at Eton, the Coventry nave window, and those in the so-called 'Fish' Church at Stamford, Connecticut are all impressive vertical manifestations of line in architectural structure. The architectural line at Audincourt is dominantly horizontal as a frieze is horizontal, and so also is Robert Sower's glass mural at Kennedy Airport, albeit in this instance punctuated by the delicate vertical texture of the glazing mullions.

47, 55
title page

It is relevant here to refer back to the matter of scale. The lines of essential framework may be disposed by the builder or designer according to the logical engineering of the available material (the limitations of stone are different from those of metal), and in the past these considerations tended to impose a sort of natural or organic scale of interval between voids and solids, glass and structure. One

New York, Kennedy Airport, American Airways Terminal. Robert Sowers.

senses that in a classic Perpendicular window such as Eton College Chapel or St. George's, Windsor, the division of the total area into nine vertical spaces by eight mullions, linked horizontally by transom and tracery, is somehow right *organically*. With the modern reinforced concrete technique, however, the load-bearing thrusts can be disposed in such a way as to leave very large and often quite arbitrary voids into which modern glazing technology can fit large sheets of plate glass uncluttered by smaller intervals of framework. This leaves the artist free from any imposed scale and throws him back on his own innate sense of interval or punctuation though he is still limited, it must be admitted, by the sizes of panels which can be conveniently handled for fixing.

The deliberate asymmetrical placing of the glazing bars in the Tudeley window neither assists nor frustrates engineering requirements. Some division was necessary to hold the optimum size of a glazed panel, but the artist has presumably disposed them unequally in order to 'throw' the spectator from preconceived ideas about a classically shaped window. It could be argued that this makes the bars intrude into the picture plane—instead of merely dividing it. The ability to cast very large glass slabs or *dalles*,[1] such as those known as 'dalles de Boussion' has led, for instance in the Church of St. Joan of Arc near Belfort, to an over-large glazing scale, and what is really a very large Sanctuary window looks paradoxically small until one sees the size of the seated figures beneath it. Such a reaction is founded on the observer's coming with an inherited sense of 'pane' size (in the same way as he looks at a building with an inherited sense of brick size) and if the pane size is very large, he unconsciously sees the window as smaller than it is in order to bring it to a more human scale. If this hypothesis is correct, it means that we appreciate, knowingly or unknowingly, certain linear fundamentals about a window even before we concentrate our attention on its content.

Having been drawn into the architectural frame of the window and into the scale of breakdown (the glazing bars, panes, etc.) which it contains—whether this is done with conscious awareness of its importance as a skeleton or otherwise—we next see how well or ill the ligaments and muscles of the interior lines connect, articulate, flow, or activate the subject. There are some cases where the fenestra-

Belfort, Saint Joan of Arc church. Jean-Luc Perrot.

---

[1] Slabs of glass, normally 300 × 200 mm, cast about 35 mm thick.

tion imposed by the architect is so dominating that the depth and expression of the artist's linear composition can only complement, by subtle extension in an abstract way, the structural elements already containing the glass in their powerful grip. Such a case is the 'Fish' Church at Stamford. Here the artist can do no more than set a colourful 'sky' behind the forest of artificial trunks and branches—a similar effect, in fact, to that which can be seen from observation of light striking through a wood. A less dominant, but still powerful fenestration can be seen at Coventry where the artists concerned adopted several devices such as extension, complement, or contradiction in an attempt to come to terms with the imposed grid of vertical and horizontal stonework. The first device—that of extension can be seen from the detail of one of Keith New's green windows where strong black lines, almost as thick as the mullions, seem to grow out of the transom and curve up into an uncoiling spring shape from which the eye is taken down to the black circles below containing a horizontal and a vertical line respectively. This same example also shows elements of complement and contradiction. The light, in plant-like shafts rising in the outer lights to merge and grow upwards through the window, may be said to complement or reflect in reverse the black mullions. There is contradiction, on the other hand, in the black border of the green circle appearing in the top of the centre lights and in the dark diagonal shafts of the arrows which break into it, cutting across the vertical/horizontal fret of the stonework. The virtue of New's solutions, when seen in the window as a whole, lies in the preservation of a fine lyricism of subject—spring, youth, growing things—which does not fight the black grid imposed on it but uses it like a kind of trellis.

As a demonstration of *complement* we need no more than refer once more to the Jesse window at Chartres. Here there are strips of 73 blue roughly equivalent to the thickness of the iron ferramata, rising first as the limiting edge of the border and reflecting exactly the shape of the window. They are then used as semi-circular loops to contain the figures flanking the main subject of the Kings as far as the topmost division of the bars when they swing back into the border to allow the figure of Christ a more important space. The essentially linear nature of the subject—the tree—moves upwards, carrying the main figures with it, culminating in branches whose terminals are a series of roundels that complement the coiled stem

Above: *Coventry Cathedral, Golden window (Man side). Lawrence Lee.*

Left: *Coventry Cathedral, Green window (Man side, detail). Keith New.*

Kingsclere, Berkshire.
'Benedicite omnia opera'.
Lawrence Lee.

motif which occurs above each lift of the saddle bars. In the modern example, 'Benedicite omnia opera', the vertical strips of lightish glass are used as an internal *contradiction* to the generally horizontal lines of the landscape behind. In this example the subject is expressed in the active ascending vertical lines terminating in the sun contrasted with the passive lines of the landscape, folded horizontally by geological forces and richly covered with vegetation.

A variant of the principle of contradiction may be found in the broader forms of a window and is quite common in historical multi-light windows which use rows of figures to read as a horizontal band of tone and colour across the lights. Matisse has used the same method in the window behind the choir stalls at Vence, blocks of colour in individual lights fusing together when seen as a whole and forming continuous waving bands of blue, green, and yellow. Having said all this about extension, complement, and contradiction, and looking again at the examples, we would be perfectly correct in saying that all three are interchangeable terms stating the same thing from different starting points. All extensions, if properly handled, are at once both contradictory and complementary or have greater or lesser degrees of these things: in the last resort all must be complementary to the architecture, the internal form, and the subject. For instance, it will be remembered that there was an implied criticism of Chagall's Tudeley window in referring to the uncomfortable method of breaking up areas of colour with leads. My own opinion is that these leads have been regarded as necessary evils to be designed somehow into a linear pattern and in consequence they have become conscious and distracting. All stained glass artists have to tackle this problem, but in more traditional work the formal compositions seldom demand the large interrupted areas of one colour that one often finds so vital in work composed from a painter's point of view. How strange it is that, faced with bothersome lead lines and the problem of what is to be done with them, Matisse seems instinctively to have adopted the true glazier's trick of making them surround his colours and his images and letting any other physically necessary breakdown of the glass occur in deliberate horizontal lines or apparently arbitrary and unconscious breaks—thus, in effect, losing them as compositional lines and turning them into a part of structure.

The impact of linear considerations so far discussed, though vitally important, is not so immediate to the eye as the more delicate, but ultimately more artistically expressive use of line in the painted content of the window. As I have said in another work:[1]

The primary function of glass painting is unquestionable—to extend and clarify an image already established in the colour and leading pattern. The

[1] *Stained Glass,* Oxford Paperbacks Handbooks for Artists, p. 68.

persistent lines of lead can only be extended, complemented, by something which is itself linear: a form of drawing moving from dense and immobile black line into the energy and eroding power of light.

This is a stark statement of the classical attitude to painted lines on glass. It is demonstrated with great assurance and simplicity in the example from Fladbury. In the lines of the drapery of the Child the essential form is made by powerful lines from which branch finer, tapering, sprung lines to suggest modelling over the volume of the body. All that has to be expressed in both form and gesture is synthesized with a degree of sophistication which makes nonsense of the old idea that Medieval artists 'couldn't draw'. Great glass painting has an extreme economy of means and intention which nevertheless bewitches us with its beauty and personality. In this it is comparable to such acknowledged works of art as Chinese calligraphy, the Tassili cave paintings, or even Picasso drawings. The final condemnation of later naturalistic glass painting which tried to copy academic painting, can be stated as a complete derogation of the function and importance of painted line in the effective extension of line pattern already established in the lead and bar structures of the window. One has only to compare the Fladbury detail with, for instance, that illustrated in the margin on page 89.

A more detailed examination of painted line will be appropriate in the chapter dealing with glass painting, but it will be important to remember that however we may be enchanted with the beauties and subtleties of the glass painting art, strong line work, resolute even in delicacy, is as indigenous to traditionally leaded windows as the leads themselves.

Chinese drawing.

Tassili cave painting.

Discussing colour without the help of a great number of colour reproductions would seem almost impossibly irksome in the case of coloured windows. There are many qualities in which we can delight when studying a good black and white photograph of a painting—its composition, tonal control (to some extent), modulation of form and drawing—but without colour a stained glass window loses the first reason for its existence. Nevertheless I shall attempt to show how we may gain something important from the very absence of colour. Without the distraction of a great many colour plates the reader will, I hope, be led to three things. First, to the better understanding of the vital place that *tone* has in the interplay of colours of light, dark, and medium strength; second to a classification of the strength or weakness of the linear structure and enrichment without which colour might be nothing more than a flabby arrangement of odd shapes and third, to the seeking out of the windows to which I refer—if only to confirm or deny the argument which I shall put forward. I think some argument is almost inescapable, for I cannot hide my considered opinion that many windows which command a first unthinking admiration, do so by an appeal to the emotional impact of coloured light while, hiding behind this appeal, are often desperate weaknesses of design, lack of tonal control, and a failure to understand the architectural or religious function of a window. In this chapter I shall hope to provide a key which may be studied with the help of an analogy as precise as its limits will allow and by which we may dimly 'see' the nature of colour as a musician can 'hear' the music written in a score.

I have mentioned emotion in speaking of the direct appeal of windows and I would not have it said that I deprecate emotion in this most visually stimulating of all arts. Stalin said that artists were the 'engineers of the soul'—a statement which, linked with hard steel ideology and bureaucratic interpretation, strikes cold against the heart; but if the same thing had been said by a poet, as a poet would intend it, it would be strangely true. If an artist is to stimulate the delicate mechanism of the soul in others, his own must first be subject to the severest discipline. Emotion may be allowed to get out of hand in private 'subjective' art (though I am not certain that this is in the ultimate analysis allowable) but in public 'objective' art it is a disaster. False emotion in this context is not only an up-surging, romantic outpouring of over-colourful images, it may be simply the feeling aroused by an image that seems more impressive because it has been made large—or as I should call it, out of scale. It may be something to do with feeling an exciting emotion about a mass of colours merely because the colours are very brilliant—or as I should again say—out of scale. In the last resort, which emotion most ministers to this 'soul'—that infinitely adaptable mechanism of aesthetic appreciation? Is it the state of auditory shock undergone when listening to a strident pop singer, or is it the experience of intense feeling held taut and disciplined in listening to a Beethoven quartet?

Of all things, colour in a window is the most critical element, not only with regard to its control by the artist, but in its power to have a life of its own once it has passed out of his hands and has been set immovably in the public place. It is no playground for ephemeral emotions but an activity in light that must be able to hold its drama, story, image, living yet controlled in a single plane—in fact, a stage without depth. So it is that, in common with some other formal arts, such as great frescoes or mosaics, Russian icons, oriental drama, and most liturgical music, great windows evince a certain austerity or withdrawn quality—an odd paradox when one considers the visual immediacy of coloured glass—and this is, I believe, because of the formal drama they have to enact in light. The effect of the irradiation of the glass as the light passes through its texture or over its surface, together with the inescapable condition of a power imposed by a remote source (the sun), gives stained glass the 'otherness' of Ravenna mosaics and, at the same time, makes all pretence at natural drama irrelevant.

It should be emphasized that the word 'surface', in the sense in which I have just used it, is linked with structure, i.e. a flat, continuous area of glass held in a single plane structure; but here the use of the word, in its more precise definition of the actual physical limit of a material, must cease when we are thinking of glass. The image of a spider's web is not a poetical metaphor—it is a fairly exact analogy: we think of the web (leads) as black against the landscape, the bits of glass filling the interstices; framed by the threads, the landscape is

61

held intangibly on the picture plane of the window. Hence, glass has the curious quality of being a pre-eminently two-dimensional art, but one which carries its substance suspended in light without contributing any immediate satisfaction of surface. Indeed, when glaziers talk of the deleterious effect of surface light, they refer to the diffusion of a strong front light on the painted side of the glass (lights switched on in a church on a dark afternoon is a typical instance) which effectively shows up the solid, tactile material of the glass but destroys its transparency.

It must be supposed that this phenomenon of the optical relationship between the eye and the surface of a two-dimensional work of art had been explored and analysed by writers on aesthetics or the psychology of perception, but I believe I am right in saying that it has not been discussed in the context of window glass. What I mean by this phenomenon can be stated thus: the physical surface is the limit that terminates a solid between itself and an observer—or, in tactile terms, the material which is touched or apprehended; this can convey, through optical laws, an impression of roughness, smoothness, dullness, or polish peculiar to the thing seen. By this we know that a painting is varnished or that a sculpture is rough or polished without having to touch them. It is by this mode of perception that we know that a painting by Cimabue must have a different surface finish from a painting by Rembrandt, that the material of the Ravenna mosaics is different from that of Fra Angelico's frescoes in San Marco. The contribution of the surface quality in the field of wall painting and decoration is often overlooked: fresco and mosaic are the only really valid media because their surfaces have a unique reaction to light, which confines their existence to, and makes them an intrinsic part of, the wall. In the case of fresco this special activity of surface can only be explained by a kind of silken sheen which develops as the wet plaster and colour dry out—the result being, in fact, a painting absorbed into a silica skin. Mosaic also, as a fabrication of innumerable little 'bricks' of ceramic and glass, has the same effect of glaze and of belonging essentially to the wall. The 'fresco secco' of northern Europe has much the same effect, though, being applied to dry plaster, it has a more chalky appearance. These media are applied direct to the wall and become part of it; so-called mural paintings done on large canvases are, by this standard, merely large paintings, and as their introduction coincided with the Renaissance

109

painters' highly developed modelling of figures and deeply recessed landscapes, they have no value as wall decoration in its strictly architectural connotation.

Mosaics and fresco lead us a little way towards the special state of stained glass in so far as they have the same dedication to the building —to an enriched expression of the wall surface by subtly remaining *on* its surface, just as iridescence on a piece of heavily corroded glass expresses the form of the glass. The distinction of glass is that when it is held up to the light the surface disappears and nothing much can be learnt from it about its tactile qualities. The Tassili rock paintings, because of the corrugations and granulations of the rock face, also have a true mural quality. Oil painting developed as an increasing movement away from the surface of the canvas into illusions of roundness and recession, of light and shade and atmosphere; as a medium it was ideally suited to this because it was infinitely adaptable to every cunning wish of the painter who felt no allegiance to the primed canvas as a material having some say in the final illusion. A number of modern painters have clearly desired a return to the conditioning of surface by material—the use of coarse unprimed canvas is an obvious example—but one feels they would be better served by a slab of hewn stone. We have yet to see paintings done direct on the wood-shuttered concrete finish of some modern interiors. They could be quite beautiful.

Before even considering the window's subject or artistic quality, we find the surface of the glass is already active with miniature dramas. There are bubbles and seams throwing odd points or streaks of light. A single shaft of sunlight may become intensely concentrated by some accident of refraction, alone among its fellows throwing a patch of light on the floor. A nearby tree may cast a filigree pattern of shadows that dance delicately across the panes. The weather itself, trapped for a moment in the proscenium arch of the window, plays white clouds across a blue backdrop, or on a foggy day lays over it a grey, mute curtain. At twilight coloured glass will act out a secret game with the fading light, some colours such as red, soon turning black, others, their painted eloquence once singing in sunlight, are now turned in on themselves and silent; and at last, with the light all but gone, the blues, in a special reaction to the physical property of light, hold their notes till the last trace of day departs. All these influences are meeting on the transparent surface of glass and the light, acting according to its peculiarities, is absorbed, modified, distorted, and finally passed through to the human retina with an impact similar to that of sounds on the human ear drum. Hence my analogy with music.

Yet analogies between art and music are usually imprecise, often derived from vague, romantic notions about art in general; though there are some common criteria—proportion, contrast, form, and so on—you cannot assert that a note is 'blue' any more than you can assert that a painting has a 'fugal' structure. Art lives in space in an instant vision of the eye; music lives in time in the progression of notes falling on the ear. Stained glass, however, has this singular and exact difference from other visual arts of being seen by direct light passing through the medium of glass and falling directly on the eye. Light waves, shifting along a part of the spectrum according to the colour of the glass they penetrate, activate the retina with direct effect, as sound waves activate the ear drum. The average coloured window will signal many 'notes' and, by virtue of juxtaposition, various mixtures of notes, or 'chords' will appear to be present in the window. This effect is reinforced by halation. These chords could be experienced as a vibrating image coming out from coloured light, similar to the vibrating aural image coming out from a source of sound, such as an organ.

In my youth operators of cinema organs sometimes 'showed off' by pulling out all the stops until the ear drum became saturated with noise. There exist windows which produce a similar babble of 'noise' on the eye. A painting cannot do this by colour alone, though it can achieve a visual hurt by using certain colours or patterns in deliberate optical antithesis. A violent, crudely coloured window may be a simple offence to the eye in a secular building; in a church it may become a double offence by inhibiting a relaxed state of mind proper to the particular ethos of the place. At the other extreme, weak or timid colouring will do a disservice by lowering the threshold of expectation to a point of rosy sentiment so that we may have the visual equivalent of a Palm Court orchestra only suited to vapid conversation over tinkling cups.

One's state of expectancy is very important in the art of appreciation. Reproductions can create false expectancies. How often do we hear someone say, 'It is a lot sharper in colour than I had expected', or 'I expected it to be a much larger window'? Both these comments may uncover actual faults or virtues in the artists' colour or design. The 'sharpness' of the glass, not revealed in a colour reproduction, may be owing to the artist's failure to understand the physical reactions of one colour on another in the actual concentration of light in voids and against the black solids of the surrounding building, or it may be merely a wilful use of a particularly 'acid' colour. On the other hand, the surprise of seeing a physically small window may be the result of the extreme skill of the artist in suggesting a feeling of intense incident in breadth over a small area so that he has successfully created that same delightful shock we experience when, after years of seeing a famous painting reproduced in books, we see it face to face and marvel how small it is after our expectation.

It may help us to pursue the analogy of music if we drop the term 'artist' in referring to the designer of a window. The maker of music is called a musician and that means what it says. A maker of windows is called a glazier—and that, too, means what it says. A musician contains sound formally, making even silence significant: a glazier contains light formally and makes it significant by the very interruption he imposes on it. In its initial impact on the eye stained glass is intrinsically abstract, producing an immediate response to an order in colour and design which may be quiet, harmonious, sonorous, or strident regardless of the subject matter. Conditioned light for a religious purpose need not require stained glass at all: the simple nineteenth-century industrial glazing of a Welsh Nonconformist chapel may enclose a truer atmosphere of worship than a church whose windows are stocked with the stereotyped piety of the Gothic Revival. For the moment, then, we are considering glass as a medium of abstract manipulation of the 'sound' of light. Later we shall see how this intimately reinforces the idea or subject of a window—or fails to do so.

There is another standard which is generally applied to windows and has its counterpart in music with an equivalent spiritual and architectural setting, namely liturgical music. It will be difficult to define this without running the risk of seeming to put both arts into a straitjacket, but I must crave indulgence for the temporary use of this standard to help out in a complex situation. It is best introduced as the *retention of the essential plane or continuity of surface*, a continuum of colour, tone, and design on a level which does not admit of any very

Haverfordwest,
Pembrokeshire,
Methodist church.

obvious emotional or naturalistic advance or recession within the
established range. Contained within this level the artist or composer
may work quite profound harmonies, dissonances, counterpoints,
etc., without appearing to move far from a given anchorage, or a
limited compass. Plainsong has an extreme limitation of movement
up and down, but its anchorage seems to be set at a pitch from which
a series of sounds can evoke a quite strong but elevated emotion.

Many people are familiar with Grechaninov's 'Credo' which creates the most moving sound from what is virtually one note. Composed for the Russian Orthodox liturgy, the 'Credo' consists mainly of a recital of the Creed by a rhythmic solo line in monotone, with simple but beautifully evocative support from the choir. In the same manner, windows which are practically colourless have been able to convey a quality of light and atmosphere of a very high aesthetic order. The 'Five Sisters' window in York Minster is a classic example, achieving quite beautiful harmonies by the use of various tones of white or neutral glass punctuated with fragments of colour. Though the stimulus for this extreme economy of colour is said to be the ordinance of the Cistercian Order banning decoration in their Abbeys, there can be no doubt that the glaziers took this as a challenge and introduced a sense of 'colour' into these plain grisaille windows by the use of varied whitish glasses overlaid with a filigree of paint and stain.

Likewise, the stringencies of pure economy can also give rise to some highly interesting solutions. There were probably many reasons for the greater frequency of grisaille or semi-grisaille windows towards the end of the thirteenth century. No doubt one of these was the demand for increased light, possibly linked with the development of internal sculpture and the desire to light up the increased sophistication of the vaulting. Transitions can be seen in the church of St. Urbain at Troyes and St. Pierre at Chartres. Again, the greater height of windows may have led the glaziers to concentrate the available colour into figures with rich backgrounds, set in canopy work and placed in the middle range of the lights, leaving the lower and upper parts filled with diapers of lead graced here and there with medallions of colour. The window of the life of St. Gervais in the choir of St. Ouen at Rouen is a demonstration of this device. A later example of this kind of plain glazing can be studied at Halifax Parish Church in Yorkshire. Here a number of so-called 'Commonwealth' windows whose patterns were probably derived from a Jacobean book of glaziers' draughts and set out on the workshop floor in a fairly rustic manner (for the vertical and diagonal lines are far from accurately spaced, and would be unacceptable in the modern drawing office). The result is a subtle irregularity which, combined with the irregularities in the texture of the hand-mixed whites of the glass, produces a singularly rich effect—almost as of black lace. An out-

63

standing modern example of 'colour' in this austere sense is the Church of Maria Königin at Cologne where the whole nave wall is a curtain of white and neutral glass with knots or concentrations of colour arranged as symbols. A similar scheme is used in the adjacent baptistery, and it is interesting to note that much of the glass is what is described as rolled or pressed glass—the kind often used for bathrooms or partitions on which patterns of various designs are moulded —and this catches the light in its many facets, diffusing a sparkling effect over the surface. There is a clever counterpoint of dark and light glass—the fragments above showing dark against the clear sky and those below catching the light against the dark area of the trees outside. This is a good illustration of the preservation of the essential surface of the glass against the disruptive effect of outside things. In terms of glass expressing subject, it is beautifully evocative of water— the element of baptism.

I have deliberately set the question of colour in its lowest key in order to demonstrate the importance of keeping a strong hold on the single surface of the plane of glass (or, musically, the restriction of the compass of the theme). If the restriction of surface can be accepted by the observer, it will be found a very secure base from which to begin to assess colour: he will find himself less bewitched by mere hue— the unrelated senseless babble of a mass of bright colour with which modern glass technology debauches the undisciplined glazier. He will find that much modern abstract glazing which is currently fashionable makes monotonous use of reds, blues, and yellows but lacks tonal contrast. The semi-abstract windows of Einar Forseth in Coventry Cathedral are colourful in the primary sense of being composed of fairly straightforward blues, reds, greens, and yellows, but the total effect is curiously flat and uninteresting.[1] I would suggest that a visitor to the cathedral might try the experiment of looking first at the Forseth windows and then at the so-called golden window on the baptistery side. The latter is an abstract made up entirely of painted and stained white or tinted glass and sets out to express through conditioned light the indefinable Godhead. It is anonymous in treatment, the design having been carried out by the assistants of the three artists who did the remainder of the nave windows, as a device to prevent any one artist's personal style having too much say

[1] An illustrated booklet of the windows can be obtained from the Cathedral Bookshop.

in the treatment of the glass. Forseth's windows, on the other hand, designed to express the coming of Christianity to Sweden, are highly personal, even mannered. The spectator must decide which of these two examples is the more effective. Is a stained glass window just a matter of providing a religious subject in nice bright primary and secondary colours, or is it a more complex affair of expressing profound ideas by the highly controlled use of light? It could be argued that the lack of contrast in tone of the Forseth windows is exactly what I am advocating when I talk of a 'single surface or plane of the glass' and that I am contradicting myself by commending the Maria Königin glass with its clustered symbols and glass ranging from pure white to virtual black. Though I am conscious of putting my arguments badly, it is not so much a contradiction as a paradox.

73 Another comparison may help. I have already mentioned the Jesse window in Chartres Cathedral. The construction of the ironwork gives six more or less equal divisions with a semi-circular panel at the top, and the ancestors of Christ are spaced fairly symmetrically in each panel up to the culminating figure above the springing line. There is, however, a continuous *structure*, analogous to musical structure, not only in the physical divisions of the iron-work, but in the complementary division of the pattern created by the vine, the blue curves enclosing the flanking figure and the borders. The modulation of colour from quite dark greens, purples, and reds to lightish pinks and blues is therefore suspended in a two-dimensional curtain or plane of pattern. Like the Maria Königin glass, whatever the range of lightness and darkness of the glass, we remain convinced that the window is intended as a single surface presented to the light, the whole design providing a rich pattern of dark knots of subject mixed with sparkling borders and infillings. The clustering of darks, the sparkling of lights, the concentration of colour, the shimmering cascades of whites, all act out their play across the spider's web of the structure and every piece of glass, like an individual note in a piano sonata, has its own place and importance. The varied blues are not just background but a total blue 'chord': the rich purples are not just cloaks of kings, but punctuations to indicate the triumphant progress of the image as it develops through the brilliant arpeggios of the borders. The 'drama' of the colour is not the illustrative drama of programme music but the abstract orchestration of a prelude and fugue: it is not the great crashing chords, bleak

silences, or honeyed melodies, suggesting storms, death, sorrow, or romantic love, not *Sturm und Drang*, but the vibrations of guitar strings, clear as single notes or in unison, creating passages of sound though never moving beyond that total quality of sound that the plucked string can make. It is not the distant atmospheric drama of the great sunset, but the May morning, the dewdropped spider's web suspended in front of the landscape and transforming it into an abstraction of colours within the interstices and in the same plane as its structure.

In contrast let us consider a window which demonstrates the opposite approach. The example illustrated is typical of many renderings in glass of Holman Hunt's popular painting 'The Light of the World'. Putting aside for the moment the ethics of taking an idea created by a painter and adapting it for another purpose, our concern here is with the physical effects of transcribing a painting into a stained glass window. Passing over the ineptitude which seeks to express the Christian's ultimate concept of the source of light by borrowing from a painting which, once translated into glass, must, of necessity, deny the light by which it alone could live, the very logic of the chiaroscuro necessary to pinpoint the lantern as the dramatic source of light in the painting, demands the destruction of the logic of overall transparency by which a window exists. In this case the designer of the window has made some effort to overcome the concentration of the lightest spot in the lantern by making the nimbus appear brightly illuminated and the shadows in the white robe less dramatically expressive of the single patch of light adjacent to the lantern itself than in the original painting. In fact he has really altered quite a number of things in an attempt to achieve a more decorative treatment—painting patterns on the robe, tidying up the weeds in the foreground, and adding a little red border round the nimbus—all inherited devices of the glass studio. In spite of these skills the result is lugubrious, evoking no interest specific to coloured light nor any real spiritual benefit other than a vague second-hand piety. In terms of our *schema* for what a window ought to be, our essential picture-plane to contain light in a special sort of way, this window demonstrates how far glass-painters have been prepared to go in perpetuating an entirely false concept of stained glass.

On the principle that each piece of glass should have a place in the total orchestration—it will be seen that in this instance more than

half the area of the window is contributing no colour and no light of any significance and could almost be replaced by cardboard without attracting attention. The 'plane' has been destroyed in the endeavour to produce recession by perspective and shadow so that we are not looking at a window at all, but at a transparent painting slightly conventionalized for technical reasons and seen through a Gothic shaped hole.

If we apply the simple test that every piece of glass in a window should admit light, whether its role is significant in the main subject or more insignificant as a part of a border we shall find that depends on the designer's understanding of the relationships between all the colours he uses and their proper orchestration over the continuous surface of his composition. Even then his responsibility is not to the window alone but also to the architecture into which it is set and from which it draws its only sanction.

As a conventional and well-known setting out of these classic relationships we may take the cathedral of Chartres while, curiously, only 32 kilometres away we may find its antithesis in the Chapelle Royale de Saint-Louis at Dreux. If Chartres is Christ, Dreux is Antichrist. Enshrining the tombs of the d'Orléans family and built to the concepts of a different age from that of Chartres, the Chapelle Royale is a morgue of dead sculpture and glass: skill with material is driven to the extreme of naturalism where the stone and glass no longer have any life of their own but, like waxworks or photographs, reflect only what they represent. The windows (executed by the Sèvres factory) depict religious scenes with realistic modulation of anatomy, clothing, and landscape, accurate perspective and dramatic composition involving enormous contrasts in colour and tone, mostly confined to a single group and unrelated to the shape of the window. All light is damped down by paints and enamels skilfully applied to large pieces of glass and the necessary evil of the leads is effectively disguised, where they must occur, by very deep shadows. For the visitor, the custodian of this extraordinary place will switch on a hidden light behind the 'Crucifixion' window and the whole thing takes on a brownish glow, giving the effect of a Rembrandt painting complete with highlights of pure white on helmets, spears, and other metal objects. We see here how the art of the glazier has reached its ultimate perversion by the art of the glass painter. That reserved surface, which all art must maintain between itself and the

74

observer, is broken down by an invitation to wallow in the drama and
pathos of a religious tragedy displayed without reference to those
deeper abstract harmonies of light, colour, and structure so pre-
eminently demonstrated at Chartres. In terms of colour this extreme
example underlines the essential argument, namely that criteria of
colour in a painting are different from those applied to a coloured
window. What is right for Rembrandt is not right for the glass-painter,
and vice versa. This seems obvious; but, after several centuries of
degradation of stained glass and false values, it was not an artist but a
lawyer with an antiquarian interest in 'painted windows' (as they
were then called) who put his finger on the trouble.

Charles Winston published his *Hints on Glass Painting* in 1847[1] and he was at pains to show how medieval glass gained its brilliance from having portions of each piece of glass left clear of paint for the full transmission of light, while shadows were granulated by stippling (rather than smearing) and hatching (rather than blacking) the darkest parts. This was in contrast to the glass of his times which had 'dullness and opacity arising from want of clear lights and transparent shadows'. Combined with this misapplied skill of painting was the current use of flat, dull coloured glass chosen mainly to give the sombre 'historic painting' effect. With the advent of better made, clearer glass, stimulated by the William Morris movement, a purer colour and light began to pervade church windows. A Pre-Raphaelite window, for all its dated quality, can always be picked out among duller nineteenth-century companions by this glowing transmission of light and it will continue to glow on a late winter afternoon when the others have become little more than a dense, muddy screen, hardly recognizable as glass.

We have had, in our discussion of colour, looking over our shoulders and occasionally participating, several other actors in the drama of a window. Principal among these is one we call 'design'—in fact, the whole play would fall to pieces without this first among equals. For we have really been talking about the design of colour—the flesh and blood of the hidden skeletal structure or 'design' of an assemblage of glass held by leads and saddle bars in the architectural zone we call a window. All the illustrations in black and white have had to stand up to the analysis of structure and tone without the help of actual colour. In this context it is interesting to note that even in an abstract modern window it is still possible to upset the essential continuum or surface of glass as effectively as any eighteenth-century glass-painter, even if the images are not figures, buildings, and landscape in naturalistic recession but ill-chosen depths or lightnesses of colour or tone in relation to each other. In some modern windows there are badly massed shapes or areas of intense colour, either at the top or at the bottom, more or less unrelated to the architectural form, which have the same effect of making 'holes' through the glass wall of the window—of asserting a highly personalized statement

[1] Charles Winston, *An enquiry into the difference of style observable in Ancient Glass Painting, especially in England, with Hints on Glass Painting.* Oxford, J. H. Parker, 1847.

Derby Cathedral. One of the two windows by Ceri Richards.

without apparent regard for what Léger called 'the integrity of the picture plane'.

A critic of the argument I have tried to present might with some justification contend that what I am saying is that the maintenance of the two-dimensional austerity of surface is a deliberate archaism—as though a musician would argue that liturgical singing should not move far from the plainsong chant. Though I would resist this doctrinaire straitjacket—which I only applied to get the argument under some sort of control—there is in it, I believe, a truth worthy of consideration.

I feel the recent emphasis on the idea of *participation* in drama, art, music, religion, etc., to be a mistake—at least in the degree to which it is pushed in some quarters. When the individual human consciousness is brought into public association with other human beings in what we call groups, congregations, audiences, or spectators, it cannot achieve its full *inner* potential of participation unless its outer shell is protected by some convention of behaviour appropriate to the thing to be experienced. These conventions prevent the invasion of the psyche by other people's emotions, thoughts, or actions irrelevant to the purpose of the group activity. The decent, orderly liturgy of the Church of England is one such convention admirably suited to many English people. The richer liturgy of Latin countries serves a different temperament. The generally subdued behaviour of spectators at a cricket match, and the massed vocal encouragement at a football match, are both appropriate to their particular expectancy—or what the spectator is prepared to act out in unison with his fellows as part of his enjoyment. The argument for the exceptional controls to be experienced in what is done on the surface of a window or on the surface of the liturgy is not to kill emotion but to allow the energy of emotion space and time to lift itself free from the gravity of the petty, the sentimental, or the morbid 'earth' in which our immediated physical self is held. The windows of Chartres or Canterbury, the liturgical music of Palestrina or Monteverdi are designed to do just this, as are the Matisse windows at Vence or Britten's St. Nicholas Cantata.

Looking at the typical church furnisher's crucifix (drops of blood painted red) or hearing a congregation wallowing in 'When I survey the wondrous Cross' do no more than stir expected and vaguely gratifying feelings of remorse or penitence. And looking at a typical memorial window we are not expected to do more than admire the noble but very physical airman, the fine eagle of the R.A.F., and the accurately realized propeller, and be left with a pleasant feeling that because they are in a window they are somehow sanctified. Sanctification is in the glass, not in the subject. The two angels illustrated may be expressions of an idea of unearthly beings (common to all

Contrasted angels: Chartres (above) and an illustration in a 19th century church furnisher's catalogue (below).

78

Derby, Rolls Royce Works, RAF memorial window. Hugh Easton

mythologies) in this case expressed as a Christian concept. And they no longer may be credible to enlightened man. Yet if one were asked which of these two reproductions most effectively conveys the Christian concept of angels ('He maketh his angels spirits and his ministers a flaming fire'[1]) I think we would have no doubt that the Chartres angel wins hands down, expressing as it does an incandescence of energy beautifully transmuted into glass and being above all infinitely removed from the immediacy of shallow sentiment conveyed by a man or woman who happens to have wings.

[1] Ps. 104.

CHAPTER 8   Painting

I recall some words of an art critic in the studio when we were making the Coventry windows. At some point in our discussion he said, 'You have all these jewel-like colours, all this marvellous glass —why on earth do you smear that dirty brown paint over them?'— or words to that effect. In his own terms, that of easel painting, one could say that painting on the glass was an essential development of the medium to give expression to that which could not be expressed simply by colour and lead lines, i.e. faces, hands, feet, drapery, and all other kinds of detail necessary to the imagery; or that some stopping down or control of the intensity of light was desirable, especially taking into account the tendency for some colours to behave differently from others when subject to this force; or that, as a result of the interplay of these functions, a particular skill in delineation, developed with the calligraphic verve we admire in the best pottery painting, should be a thing of evident delight—even to purist critics.

One of the problems in this type of confrontation is a physical one. In the studio one is too near the materials and the rather brutish devices of glazing. But the same critic, walking round Canterbury or York, would scarcely think of making the remark reported above. It would be unlikely to occur to him because of the overriding 'presence' of the windows as a complete statement. In the workshop the whole fragmented process is too close, too coarse in its impact, to allow a proper judgement. Though there is some pleasure in 'seeing how it's done', most people are confused, seeing means and ends in the wrong order.

It is impossible to begin a purely aesthetic discussion of glass painting. We are likely to bedevil ourselves with a terminology which means quite different things to different readers. Even connoisseurs of fine art may think that 'painting' means putting the colour into or onto the glass, and the presence of a kiln in the studio seems to support the idea of materials being melted or in some way processed. Others, though vaguely realizing that the main colours are already fused in the original making of the sheets of glass, are nevertheless obsessed by the notion of a secret, medieval craft and look for mysteries in painting where none exist. Generally, the best informed visitors rest content with gazing at the beautiful colours without any clear idea of the part that glass painting plays in the final effect of a window. A complete explanation of the technique pure and simple, cannot be given here, but a general definition may be helpful as a framework of the 'how' on which to expand the 'why'. Bernard Rackham's statement on the subject is as good as any.

It is sometimes supposed that enamel painting on stained glass is a relatively late innovation, but this is a misconception. Whilst it is possible to make a patterned or pictorial window entirely of glass and leadwork, without any kind of pigment as an accessory, and such windows have occasionally been produced—rather as a *tour-de-force* by modern artists—this is an exceptional method, of very rare occurrence until the end of the Middle Ages. It is true that in a good stained glass window the leadwork is always not merely a container for the glass but also an integral part of the design, but the details of a picture, such as the features of a face, folds of drapery, or petals of a rosette, were from the earliest times done by means of painting with a brush in a black enamel pigment derived from iron. In order that this pigment should adhere permanently to the surface of the glass, it is necessary that it should be fixed by fusion, at a relatively low temperature, in a small oven. . . . Lines thus painted are known by the glazier as 'trace-lines'), and the delicate gradation of them with the brush as required, from dense black masses to a tapering fineness which rival the penwork in the most sensitive of 'Old Master drawings', is eloquent proof of the skill and sure-handedness of the medieval glass painter.[1]

A precise demonstration of painting in uncompromisingly straight-58 forward terms can be seen in the Fladbury panel already referred to in the section on Line (p. 59).

Examples of the early style of direct, highly conventionalized painting are to be found in many of the cathedrals in France; Le 4 Mans, Chartres, and Bourges come readily to mind, while at Canterbury the same style is seen in the famous clerestory windows. All are typical of the thirteenth century. An example often illustrated is the small panel of the prophet Ezekiel in the Victoria and Albert Museum because it is a very clear expression of the treatment of head, hand, and drapery of that period, and also because it can be studied so easily in the Museum. The same directness is still evident in the fourteenth-century east window at Eaton Bishop near Hereford,

[1] Bernard Rackham, *The Ancient Glass of Canterbury Cathedral.* Lund Humphries, 1949, p. 6.

Eaton Bishop, Hereford.
Virgin and Child
(detail). 14th century.

and this is worth seeing as a remarkably complete window of five
lights in the setting of a small parish church. Already there is a slight
humanizing of the features, and the hands, now less heraldically
displayed, begin to express more complete gestures than the flat
presentation of the fingers and thumb of the Fladbury windows

Domestic panel. Flemish, 16th century, now in the Victoria and Albert Museum.

(see page 58). There is also a less severe silhouette of figure against background, so that the static, heavenly serenity of La Belle Verrière has given way to a more bending, fluid posture in the Virgin and Child in the extreme left-hand light. This humanizing of subject continues throughout the fourteenth and fifteenth centuries, particularly in the smaller scale of windows for parish churches, until at the end of the period it begins to lose its spiritual content in increasing pictorialism. The use of complete multi-figure compositions, first in an assemblage of medallions treated in a patterned way in windows of cathedrals such as those at Bourges and Canterbury was employed from fairly early times, but later they became

vehicles for exploiting the glass painter's skill in suggesting more human situations and emotions. These are pleasant to study, even when later on they depicted scenes of purely domestic character like that in the Victoria and Albert Museum panel.

But it is not enough to say 'pleasant to study'. By continuing to write in the vein of the previous paragraph I should do no more than work over old ground more expertly tilled by scholars and historians. If the only object of our field study is to bring back a mass of material to a kind of archaeologist's laboratory, most of what I could say would be too imprecise or else irrelevant. With such objects and in such specialized conditions analysis becomes increasingly narrowed to an abstract verbal activity in which the first intention of a work of art is lost in a set of beautifully documented mental test tubes, some of which become so fascinating as to bewitch the analyst into propounding theories which ignore the real genesis of the whole work.

The argument will always go on between those who make and those who talk about what is made—and it is very useful to both parties that it should be so. I believe, however, that in the context of this Appreciation of the Arts Series we ought to instruct ourselves to *look*, filtering out as far as possible any purely mental questions about dates, styles, authenticities and so on (all that is fun afterwards), so that appreciation becomes an impulse of our physical self towards the artist's work. We must literally pick up from the very point at which the glass painter's brush left the glass, seeing what he saw as he laid it aside for firing. Supposing he was the glazier who painted the beautiful head of the Virgin, now the only surviving precious fragment of a once complete window. Looking at it, do you appreciate the blank shape of white glass with which he started? Do you hold the brush, now loaded with pigment, hovering a moment over the imagined face, and with a single, quick stroke draw in the curve of the cheek and throat? Now can you follow him with a less full brush as he deftly lines in the nose, swinging his arm and body as he turns the tip and, with perfectly controlled tapering of the line by a lifting motion, sweeps to the merest hair-line at the eyebrow? That crown—did he draw the line over the forehead and then decide to let the hair curl over it, or did he plan the hair first and complete the base line of the crown afterwards? We may think, looking at it now, that it has the appearance of inevitability and ease, but there

Head of the Virgin. English, 15th century, now in the Victoria and Albert Museum.

are hundreds of little decisions to be made, even in painting a small head. If, for instance, he did the hair and bottom line of the crown before the upper part, did it influence the extraordinary swinging curve of the upper line, running from one side of the glass to the other, happily ignoring all formal perspective? I sense in the abandon of the crown a kind of relief. He might have completed the face in one shot and felt rather elevated that it had come off right first time, or he may have had several goes at it (nothing is easier to erase than window glass paint) and, like a tennis champion whose opponent has driven him to deuce, finally pulled off the winning shot. After it is done, the brush is loaded once more and the black masses beneath the leaves of the crown are blocked in and, when it is dry, the intermediate jewels and delicate stars are scratched out with a pointed stick, breaking the heaviness of the black masses and retaining the general fineness of the painted image. The matting (or shading) on this head is very economical. The painter may have used vinegar in this tracing paint, which after a day's drying, hardens sufficiently to allow the application of light shading with paint mixed only with water and gum. There are moments of anxiety when this is applied and gently smoothed out with the badger softener. Did the apprentice grind in enough vinegar to the tracing paint? If not—away go all those beautiful lines and the whole thing must be done again. If his nerve fails, the painter might sometimes fire in the tracing and leave himself free to apply his matts knowing that, if they are wrong, he can clean off and re-apply as much as he likes. Perhaps he was so skilled that the head 'dropped off the end of the brush', as we say, leaving the painter rather pleased with himself that he could bring off such a charmingly wistful-looking girl with so few lines and tones.

By now, I hope, we have entirely rid our minds of the suggestion, often unconsciously impregnated by sentimental references to 'simple medieval craftsmen', that we have been looking at some rather crude and unsophisticated form of drawing and painting. From the very earliest known examples the painted image was struck with a coinage already assured, already abstracted to a monumental 'readability', already the foundation of a currency not finally devalued for another five centuries. Before Cimabue was working, the windows for Augsburg, Chartres, Canterbury, and Bourges had been installed; before Fra Angelico was born the great new east window at Gloucester Cathedral had been made—a glazier's window if ever there was one,

Left: *Montreal, Church of St. Andrew and St. Paul. Head of St. Columba. Lawrence Lee. (Photographed before leading.)*

Right: *Little Malvern, Worcestershire. Fragment of a woman's head. 15th century. Note loss of painting due to the window being re-leaded with the paint side out.*

for it is almost certain that the stonework was created for the monumental scheme of the glass. And Van Eyck was in mid-career while John Thornton of Coventry was working on the superb east window for York Minster. Though over these five centuries the development of glass painting was towards greater naturalism, it is remarkable that the irrefutable convention of two dimensionality was so long sustained and enriched and only finally lost when the glass painter capitulated to the ideals of the oil painter. It is not a bad record for an art and it is one in which English glaziers can claim a major part—indeed—in some aspects of fourteenth and fifteenth-century glass painting they are unique. Robert Sowers has said: 'in Canterbury at the end of the twelfth century and throughout England of the later middle ages were created some of the finest windows of all time. English fifteenth-century stained glass perhaps contains the most pertinent clues to the legitimate revival of the art in a key light enough to be consonant with the demands of present day architecture. '[1]

[1] Robert Sowers, *The Lost Art* (Introduction). Lund Humphries, 1954, p. 10.

Westham, Sussex, East window. Fragments of the original window (c. 1420) can be seen within the main light.

Remember this when with binoculars you delight in the discovery of some odd fragment remaining in a tracery light, painted when Chaucer was writing the Canterbury Tales, and now a sad remnant from centuries of destruction, neglect, and, perhaps (a final disgrace), being bedded with a Victorian pious 'trade' replacement.

Lest we should think that glass painting, in its proper use, had died out completely by the seventeenth century, we should not overlook occasional examples of authentic painting to be found in secular

situations, notably Swiss domestic glass and heraldic panels in many historic country houses. These works have great skill and directness and they evince a genuine understanding of the explicit use of line and tone to express all that is necessary on the surface of the glass. They have not succumbed to the (then) current use of painting on church glass as a means of pictorial chiaroscuro. The last faint trace of the true glass painter's art may be seen in some surviving Victorian panels or fan-lights. Another stream of painting began with the revival of interest in the Middle Ages which culminated in the Gothic Revival of the last century. This expressed itself mainly in attempts by 'trade' studio glass painters to copy the painting techniques of the fourteenth- and fifteenth-century glaziers. They were lifeless, stereotyped, utterly without conviction, and almost any parish church in Britain can provide examples such as that illustrated. So another start was made, this time by genuine, mainly freelance artists, who had been inspired by the William Morris movement to establish a use of painted line and tone which, while acknowledging the two-dimensional dictates of the window, would evolve from a truly personal form of drawing. Inevitably the windows of this period are stamped with the designs and forms of the Pre-Raphaelite masters Morris and Burne-Jones, but for all their dated quality we must credit them with a sincere

Above: *Leeds, Yorkshire. Window formerly in All Hallows with St. Simon. 19th century.*

Right: *Christ Church, Oxford, Pre-Raphaelite window (detail).*

attempt to put glass back on its original road. When you come across windows from studios in this tradition they are characterized by a quality of light, colour, and painting which at least enhances the light of the church and they glow pleasantly in contrast to their dismal fake Gothic companions.

From Burne-Jones to the beginnings of what we generally call 'modern stained glass' there are hundreds of individual attempts to re-establish 'tradition'. The contribution of a man like Martin Travers was, perhaps, of special consequence in that he taught us really to *look* at the early glass to clear from our minds the clutter of much current medievalism, artistic posturings, bogus theories, and desiccated scholarship. We see, therefore, in his work and in that of his immediate followers, a general simplicity of design and colour, clear use of line and a little tone in painting, and often a charmingly casual attitude in the use of saints, symbols, heraldic emblems, etc., which in most of the work of his contemporaries was deadened by too great a respect for ecclesiastical and heraldic protocols. 'These rules do not seem to have been strictly observed, particularly by artists.' As one who was associated with him as pupil and assistant, this quotation sums up for me the necessary irreverence required in one committed to a lifetime of working for the Church.

The revival of glass painting may be seen in many forms in modern windows, but they may be conveniently broken down into two once separate streams, now partly merged. One has its source in the original study and close analysis of early glass, notably by Charles Winston, and flowed more or less within the confines of 'traditional' practice. Within this practice there are quite sharp differences between line and matt (or shading) but they roughly boil down to the use of painting to establish the image as a continuous surface over the entire window. At one end, the 'Travers School' maintained the historical use of line and tone which, however bold in its application, often gave an impression of great delicacy at the appropriate distance. At the other pole there was the 'Hogan School' seen at its best in windows he designed for Whitefriars, and this School is recognized by painting which is almost if not entirely devoid of stippled or brushed tones either as modelling of form or as patina to reduce the brilliancy of the glass. Taking, I believe, the theory of halation far too literally, they maintained that a solid black line would have its edge blurred by the erosion of light, and that this would produce an optical half-tone. In

Whitefriars Studio, detail of design by James Hogan.

some instances this heavy line would be echoed by a thinner one running parallel to it and giving a subsidiary blur amounting (so it was said) to a broader half-tone. In the heavy shadows, treated as solid black, there would be thin stick lights which expanded themselves to look like a ridge to catch the light—as in the illustration of the hand. My own view is that this system always appears hard and insensitive and, combined with the Whitefriars method of breaking the glass down to artificially small and equal sized pieces gives the impression that the window has been cut out of metal like a stencil. That strange ambiguous tension between large and small pieces of glass, black leads and delicate brown lines and dispersed tones, the contrast between areas of knotted denseness and expansive openness

Longmoor Garrison Church at Liss, Hampshire. Memorial window by Martin Travers.

Above: *Coventry Cathedral, Baptistery window (detail). John Piper, executed by Patrick Reyntiens.*

—all these subtleties are lost in a method which drives one theory to its logical conclusion without reference to the many other factors that contribute to the final plane or continuum of the window.

At this point the so-called 'traditional' schools meet the other stream which flows from the invasion of the glazier's world by artists with established reputations as painters. In general they seem to favour a primitive approach and the examples shown of the work 48, 47 of John Piper and Evie Hone are typical. They are saying, in effect, 'leave the glass to express itself, as far as possible, as an abstract of colour and subject and add only enough broad, even crude line and smear to convey the bare bones of the image or to provide a black and white texture unobtainable in the glass itself'. The principle is explained by Patrick Reyntiens, who has executed Piper's designs.[1] After speaking of the first method of painting, which I have called the 'Travers School', he outlines the alternatives: '. . . the other [the second method] is by starting with the clear glass, and only putting on as much paint as is needed to qualify and subdue, and to guide the essentially glittering surface of the glass.' He goes on to say:

The first method is less spontaneous, but produces an effect of great integration and firmness of design, and it is interesting that it is used more by those artists who are attracted by extremely clear and firm linear design. Great delicacy in the use of successive tonal washes can produce an extremely sombre and rich effect. The second method, which I favour, is more spontaneous, leaves more to chance and accident, and gives a heightened play and glitter to the surface of the glass. Moreover, it does not look dull or faded in back light or artificial light. At distance, the matt system [the first method] window holds its light on the window plane and holds it in reserve; whereas the free painted window is more inclined to halate and shower its light on to the surrounding masonry and the floor.

Other examples of this mode of 'large brush' attack are seen in the 9 work of Max Ingrand and Georges Rouault. On the other hand, 42 Marc Chagall in the Jerusalem and Tudeley windows and the artists 54 of the Coventry Nave windows express a preference for the controlled line and matt solution.

The conclusions we may draw from the use of such different ideas about painting can be summarized conveniently, but in no sense exhaustively. (1) There is a gradual historical growth from simple,

[1] Patrick Reyntiens, *The Technique of Stained Glass*. Batsford, 1967.

powerful linework, as at Augsburg, with a little supporting matt, to an increasing delicacy and expressive use of line with matting growing in sophistication and coverage of the glass until it eventually dominated the line in its efforts to achieve naturalistic modelling. (2) The nineteenth-century revival period gave rise to attempts at copying the technique of the Middle Ages, mostly in a hard, un-sympathetic way, and the beginning of the efforts to apply to glass the more personal, often eccentric styles of genuine artists. (3) The modern development reflecting firstly the work of stained glass artists who have been trained in the so-called traditional studios but who have evolved an authentic style which, however modern in idiom, is based on the belief that certain values of colour and light control are timeless and cannot be wilfully ignored; and secondly, the use of painting to impose the personality of painters (whose established reputations have already made their strong imprint on the public consciousness) on glass which in design, colour, and use of leads may pay scant heed to supposed historical values—one of which has been a kind of anonymity in deference to architectural harmony.

Perhaps Matisse was right, in the present state of confusion, to go straight back to the start and, with his unerring flair, to do a simple glazing job with colour and lead alone.

My own attitude to the problem is best summed up by something which I wrote some years ago:[1]

In looking at a fine piece of glass painting—from the distance intended—one is seeing something which is more than or different from the actual physical drawing on the glass. A convincing shadow under an eyebrow may be no more than the thickening of a line protected from halation by a slight matt: the highlight of a nose no more than a slender 'stick light' softened by flooding light. This deliberate committal to light and the equally deliberate ju-jitsu-like use of the very force which seems to override it, is the authentic art or 'mystery' of glass painting. After thirty years of struggle I still find myself baffled by the intricacies of this skill; and most glass painters will tell you the same thing. We all worship the same fourteenth-century god, yet not only do we fall short of the glory, but we seem, on our glass, actively to deny what we most piously assert.

[1] *Stained Glass*. O.U.P., pp. 68–9.

CHAPTER 9   Design

The word 'design' has endless interpretations. Here we are only concerned with that state of prediction, starting in the mind of the artist, which dictates all that will happen as the commission grows from sketch to cartoon, cut line to glass, glass to fired paint work, and finally to leaded panels set in an opening. Until comparatively recent times the conventional idea of design was rather mundane. To me as an art student in 1924 the word 'design' meant one day a week for first-year students spent in making patterns from historical sources and the adaptation of such things to endpapers or schemes of decorative tiles, and even this was a concession in an establishment which believed that drawing, painting, and sculpture were in an infinitely higher category than that to which 'design' was attached, namely applied art. Evidence of this attitude is all too apparent in church windows of the period and even to the present day.

Design in the sense it will be used here is something very different. It is a conformity to the imagined form of the original concept— painting, sculpture, window, sonata, or poem—arrived at by intuitive, internal disciplines. It is not a conformity to a concept imposed by external stereotypes of ideas or disciplines. External *physical* conditions are, in the case of stained glass, always imposed, and to these can be added intellectual and spiritual conditions which, like the frame of the window, induce a particular frame of mind. I think we are right to expect the artist to accept a 'frame of mind' as a necessary condition of stained glass, but we have no right to dictate what this frame of mind should eventually produce or to make predictions within it for the artist. Degrees of constriction are natural to commissions involving public architecture, and artists accept or fight against their implication with degrees of good humour, impatience, or even guile. Work for churches is particularly beset with hazards.

'The caprice or want of knowledge of the employer are too often found to over-rule the really correct view . . . of the artist. Artists are made to commit solecisms against their wish and their sober judgement. . . . A morbid taste for pretty pictures; excessive colouring . . . .'[1] This is the artist's hazard.

[1] W. Warrington, *History of Stained Glass*. 1835.

*Great Malvern,
Worcestershire. Detail
from the Creation
windows. 15th century.*

'The interior of the episcopal church here is rather elegant, with the exception of a large window of painted glass which costs 500 l., and is in vile, tawdry taste.'[1] The spectator's hazard.

These comments, coming from lay people in a period contemporary with one of the lowest ebbs of this art, are evidence of a minority that did not succumb to the prevailing conventions. Both were, in fact, critical of *design* as then conceived.

I have spoken of the 'threshold of expectation' (p. 65). The artist must always raise the expectancy of the client, for even the best patron in the world cannot foresee what the artist will do; he can only have the faith, by a knowledge of his former work, that he will do something significant. Above all, he will know that the artist's design must be an integrated whole and not a collection of items paraded in public for the glorification of the patron or his family, 'design' being mainly a set of devices for stringing them together.

The worst kind of artist (or the artist in his worst moments) will do little more than his client expects. In religious art there exists a double threshold, not only an artist and patron influenced by their inherited prejudices about art, but, often unconsciously, they are a prey to inherited prejudices about religion. Thus the brief presented to the artist may be precise or it may be open; conservative, un-informed, sectarian, radical, informed, or humanist, and there need not be any vice or virtue in these states in themselves. Artists can draw sustenance from the strangest composts of human fallibility.

The design, or imagined concept, begins to work in a state of tension between raised or lowered expectancies. By appealing to the simple physical characteristics of a window the artist will defeat a client who wants an impossibly flamboyant subject (an expectancy unsuited to the material) as it is easy to demonstrate that some subjects, demanding by their very nature a degree of symmetry, are inappropriate to a two-light window, or to show that an essentially two-figure subject is awkward in a three-light opening.

Design begins at the first meeting of those concerned with a project, the artist metaphorically feeling his way into his employer's mind as he feels his way (literally) into the masonry when surveying and measuring the material 'frame'. Already the unspoken demands of scale, colour, and incident will be developing as a filament of

*Matlock, Derbyshire,
parish church. Adam and
Eve. 19th century.*

[1] Anna Jameson, *Winter Studies and Summer Rambles in Canada.* 1839.

coloured light, vague grouping of complex incident contained in simple areas of light, proportions, masses, movements—even some details may begin to form as suggested or invented subject matter informs and modifies the first impression. This is all to do with the 'frame of mind' as the necessary containment of creative energy. Inevitably the next hazard is *subject matter*.

In *The Christian Faith in Art*[1], Eric Newton begins his contribution with these words:

It is arguable—and, indeed, as little as fifteen years ago it would have been fashionable to argue—that to consider the visual arts from the point of view of their subject matter was to misunderstand the nature and purpose of art itself; that a work of art . . . was an expression of its maker's temperament, his sense of form and colour, his preference for complexity or simplicity, modified a little by the natural behaviour of his chosen medium, and modified still further, in the cases of objects with a function, by the purpose to be served, but nevertheless primarily a communication of the artist's own visual discoveries. . . . I am convinced that such an argument, though it contains a half-truth, is essentially untenable. If I believed it I would certainly not regard it as reasonable to think of 'Christian Art' as a valid category, for it is a category that imposes on the artist not a 'subject' but a state of mind and a set of emotional attitudes that are of primary importance and must govern the whole of his creative process.

First let it be said that some artists are as irrationally fixed in a determination to avoid subject matter, or, at best, to include it only as an irrelevant concession, as some clients are equally determined in their view that subject matter is all that is necessary to a design.

If an entirely abstract window is a correct solution, properly enriching part of the general intention of the building, that is its subject matter—if you like—the matter (environment) to which it is subjected. A pictorial window executed with a high degree of naturalism and portraying a pious anecdote may on the other hand entirely thwart the intention of the architecture, making a luminous area suddenly trivial when it should have been withdrawn and held in harmonious detachment with the mysterious volume of the building. The Comper window in Canterbury is a sad example of this negative weakening of architectural mass. In this case the subject matter, however socially or religiously appealing, is as irrelevant to the true purpose of the window as is the cargo to a

[1] by Eric Newton and William Neil. Hodder & Stoughton, 1966, p. 10.

ship that has been sunk. The 'modern' approach, believing abstract art to be somehow sacrosanct because it *is* abstract, is devoid of subject and can be just as insensitive to the demands of a building as the example just quoted.

I cannot help thinking that the large area of almost white glass in the centre of the Baptistery window at Coventry exerts a severe strain on the continuity of the window structure, 'the composition culminating centrally in a clear blaze of golden light' as Sir Basil Spence describes it.[1] A 'blaze' taking place in a window which is mainly of rich, darkish colours with some heavy painting is precisely the disruption of the architectural continuum of which I have spoken in earlier chapters and it seems to me that, in this case, the subject matter is nothing more than the deliberately theatrical effect of violent light contrast. If, as I believe, it does a disservice by denying a connected sequence and activity of light over a total plane of the window, the suggestion that the dramatic hole of light in the centre represents the Holy Ghost coming in baptism is as irrelevant as Comper's portrait of the Royal Family.

It may be that, in certain circumstances, commissioning of artists with big names, merely because they are famous, is inimical to the true glazing harmony of a building. It can lead to the 'grand slam' window with vivid, eccentric treatment of subject matter, often obtruding beyond its fellows in scale, in intensity of colour, and in a general feeling of overbearing design which isolates it from the architecture. This is specially discomforting when the building is historical, when everything—façades, bays, window openings, en-richment—was conceived with a unified control, the whole developing with organic unity of scale. But it is of no concern to our argument if windows which offend this harmony are classed as modern or traditional, or whether the artist is well known or obscure. In Canterbury Cathedral there are windows in the north transept which are, to me, strikingly discordant in a positive sense, while in the opposite transept, there is the Comper window, referred to above, which is equally disruptive, but this time in a negative way. Both appear to me to ignore what the building is about. The two Bossanyi windows seem to be saying: 'We will make a concession to the surrounding twelfth-century windows by some use of the medallion

[1] *Phoenix at Coventry*. Bles, 1962.

Canterbury Cathedral,
South transept window.
Bossanyi.

shapes and patterned borders, by the use of reds and blues and figures that have something of the stance of the Old Testament worthies such as Methuselah, but we will make the medallions in our windows mere excuses for eccentric shapes to the background rather than integral to the structure of the design, and we will even upset the onlooker by doing something quite different in the companion window. You will, therefore, be cheated of a sense that

Canterbury Cathedral, North transept window. Ninian Comper (detail).

this north wall is an architectural whole and have to consider each window as an individual work of art. Furthermore, we will make our reds and blues extremely violent, and our figures very large (larger in fact than the twelfth-century prophets which were designed to be seen much higher in the clerestory) and by these tokens of bigness and brightness you will have to pay attention to us.'

In this criticism I have not made any mention of the sort of things that may or may not commend themselves to the ordinary onlooker, such as the drawing, mannerisms, shapes, rhythms, and so on. But the Comper window has a very different effect on the architecture. Here where there is a powerful wall space, deep embrasures, and a point of transition from the heavier Norman transept to the later nave, the sense of enclosure is vital as the return wall of the transept leads into the tower crossing. Comper's window merely punches a great hole of whitish light when all the expectancy is for a rich,

*Lorenz, Nuremberg.
leb and Joshua return
m the promised land
etail). 15th century.*

strongly fenestrated plane of glass to enclose the volume of transept. This window is saying, in effect, 'We have been designed to please clients who wish to honour the Crown, and the best way we can do this is to show the Royal Family in Coronation robes, posed as if for official portraits, making concessions to stained glass whenever possible by using nicely patterned robes and filling the tracery with appropriate heraldry, but the royal portraits are far too important to be left to mere designers, so we have employed a portrait painter to do them. You must forgive us if the heads are in some cases a little too big for their bodies (painters are not very used to things like the monumentality of full-sized cartoons) but you must admire the great accuracy of detail in the crown and other achievements. We are not concerned with the architecture of the transept wall, the presentation of Royalty is the main thing and we have done this by making a nice light picture in the available space. We do not wish to offend the expectancy of the Establishment.'

In the ideal solution, function, form, and subject are indispensable to each other. When we listen to Schubert's 'Winterreise' we are not separately aware of the melody of the song, the words sung, and the accompaniment. We only know that there is a unity of form (not necessarily conscious in the hearer), in the way the theme expresses the words, and how the accompaniment enfolds both. One has only to recall the treatment of Schubert's songs in the once popular 'Lilac Time' to realize that this unity of form has been destroyed by overloading *subject* with sentimentality, making the appeal merely the comfortable, romantic idea—not the intense recollected *experience* which the original composition evokes. But consider the contrast of two paintings which have religious themes. Millais's incident in the workshop at Nazareth need not at first glance be a religious painting at all, for only our inherited knowledge tells us that the figure of the woman is probably the Virgin Mary. We are attracted to all the detail of the workshop, the tools, planks, and shavings, and the human interest of the incident which (if we have a little Christian background) suggests a prophecy of the Crucifixion in the symbolism of the cut palm of the Christ Child. None of this makes it a religious creation in the dynamic sense of my argument. It is an illustration of a pretty little idea which becomes superficially religious by mental and visual associations, bringing with them a vague assurance that 'Mother will make it better' and 'We are terribly concerned for your hurt'. This is nothing much to do with real religion in anybody's language. Unfortunately it is all too often the tepid starting point of many commissions in religious art.

Contrast this with El Greco's 'Agony in the Garden'. I think it would be difficult to spend twenty minutes in front of this painting without coming away convinced that the artist had expressed a religious concept from the inside—so much so that details of rocks, bushes, drapery, as far as their natural surface qualities of texture are concerned, are unnecessary to that which he is trying to express. Rather they all, as shapes and masses, have the same part to play in the organization of the concept and appear to be deliberately interchangeable: rocks could be drapery, drapery, could be rocks, even clouds are crowding in like a cave mouth, every part of the painting maintaining this inner tension—a tension which would be dissipated if our minds were taken off to admire naturalistic treatments. This painting is not an illustration of anything, but rather an organic drama produced from its own dynamic force like an eruption from the earth itself. Without any formal religious education we sense this to be, in essence, a work of art which has to do with some fundamental God/man relationship. It is, therefore, truly religious.

To the vexed question of what modern artists do about subject matter in religious work our answer must be that an intrinsic religious expression can only come from inside the artist. Whether he has his subjects imposed by his clients or not is unimportant. An agnostic,

Christ in the house of his parents. J. E. Millais.

once he has become intensely aware, for instance, of a classically tragic situation of human will in conflict with a transcendental purpose, may produce a great work on the 'Gethsemane' theme. Conversely, a traditionally Christian artist without this prevailing conviction will only manage an allusion to a known religious incident—an illustration—not the thing itself. The critical position I have taken up may seem obvious, not in dispute among those who have an interest serious enough to read books on appreciation of the arts; but, to return to our particular subject, stained glass, we are once more confronted with difficulties. There is no doubt that much stained glass is, and was intended to be, illustration.

At this point I feel bound to qualify the word 'illustration'. It is too wide to apply without doing damage to other realms of art where illustration, more or less pictorial is not only perfectly legitimate but an art of high order. No one will contest that Cruikshank for Dickens, Tenniel for Lewis Carroll, or Shepherd for A. A. Milne have produced legitimate illustration—namely, an indefinable synthesis of visual evocation creatively adjusted to the mental evocation of the story. 'Pictorialism' is, perhaps, a better word for our purpose, especially if it conjures up the idea of naturalistic,

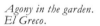
*Agony in the garden.
El Greco.*

photographic representations where everything is concentrated on the appearance of things and no thought is given to the formal values we look for in art.

102   The men carrying the grapes back from a sortie into the promised land is an apparent illustration of an Old Testament story. Yet on closer examination it ceases on several counts to measure up to what we commonly think of as pictorialism. First of all it is beautifully expressed in glass and, in direct proportion to its doing this with conviction, it becomes less pictorial; naturalistic imitation of surfaces, textures, light and shade, perspective and atmosphere are missing. Secondly, the normal concomitants of pictorialism, such as the proper costume of the period, the sun-lit Palestinian landscape with indigenous trees and correctly rendered grapes of the type that would have been growing at the time, all are missing. What we have is a composition which, although it does illustrate something in the primary sense, is very much more complex, shaped by formal values and abstractions imposed in part by the artist's understanding of the glazier's limitations, in part by his understanding of the essence of the subject. Caleb and Joshua, emissaries back from the Land of Canaan, bear a cluster of grapes to show the richness of the land. The 'haptic' exaggeration of size in the grapes is a non-realistic treatment to symbolize the potential harvest, which is a device used in the highly formalized art of primitive people and, unconsciously, in children's drawings.[1] Apart from the non-pictorial colour and linear 'drawing' imposed by the glass, paint, and lead, the presence of three floating scrolls and the introduction of the crocketed heads of a lower canopy, all tend to attach themselves to, and form part of, a surface composition. This is again emphasized by the deliberate patterning of the blue sky and the formality of the trees and by the simple, beautifully proportioned use of warm white, pale grey, green, blue, and a touch of purple. Everything combines to give an impression of a significant incident executed with the conviction of a man who knew what glass could and could not do, aware of its essential surface formality, yet able to interpret with charm and humanity. Anonymous like so many others, this glazier was from a Nuremberg workshop of about 1479 and that is all we know about him.

All that has been said about this small panel, as well as justifying

[1] Herbert Read, *Education through Art* Faber & Faber, 1943, p. 140.

the legitimate use of story-telling subject matter, also reinforces the need for the prior 'frame of mind' in the artist in making that use. A similar frame of mind must also be in the appreciator, though it generally comes to him in reverse order. Any window he studies exists first of all as a completed thing radiating its established character, and only after the expenditure of time and thought can he work his way down to the real genesis of the design. In the process there are many elements to be assessed. Assuming that the essential ordering of subject matter in relation to the true aesthetic function of the window is right, there exists within its order a number of elements we can study with profit. These are things that are common to all visual arts, but because of the monumentality of most windows, they need to be appreciated for the part they play in the rather remote (in the sense of physical distance) plane of the glass. You cannot, indeed, should not, enter into a window in the way you can 'get inside' a painting. It is a drama within a proscenium arch where a series of images presents an action in a condition of distance and light which, like the theatre, has inherited conventions of movement, gesture, emphasis, and colour to make its action 'readable' to the distant observer. We shall come to recognize a kind

Hillesden, Buckinghamshire. Detail from the life of St. Nicholas. 15th century.

Indian dancer. Compare the hands with those of the Virgin at Eaton Bishop, p. 82.

of choreography in the use of figures, not only in the expressive way the bodies are designed to demonstrate an action or an emotion, but also in the way they are grouped together. Much of what has seemed to the uninstructed observer to be mere naïvety in Gothic work can, by that standard of formalized movement we call dance, be seen as a part of the artist's conscious, fully understood display of the human figure in accordance with these inherited conventions. The position of the man falling in the carved misericord is like the position a modern ballet dancer might take up to express the idea of falling. It also happens to be an excellent solution to the enrichment of what was, after all, a simple wooden bracket. The same mime-like formalizing of a subject is present in many of the paintings of Stanley Spencer—perhaps the only modern artist actually to feel the Gothic artist's need for intensely compressed and frozen choreography. Controlled imagination of this sort produces a genuine reinforcement of the subject. Movement in a window would be disastrous if it amounted to wild restlessness, but the vision of the genuine artist, while fully accepting the material condition, sets its figures into a kind of timeless dance where, like Indian dancers, they can convey subtleties of mood and expression in the gestures which flow from the body right down through the tensile flow of arm, wrist, hand, and tapering finger.

As there can be an undisciplined sort of movement when an artist wishes to show vitality or excitement of a kind too ephemeral for a materially permanent medium like glass, so there can be a bogus variety of non-movement which parades as pious peacefulness. Static forms expressing great serenity and great finality are not achieved by sloppy, up and down lines and shapes as in the saints shown in the typically 'trade' window, but rather in an almost indefinable compression of intensity—a paradoxical use of the same force that produces the frozen movement. One senses this progressively in the greatest of all Fra Angelico's Annunciations, that in San Marco in Florence. The whole work is in a state of total control, the dynamic movement of the angel stilled by the daring use of a central column and held in by the curves of the vaultings and the arches; the inward impelling horizontals of the fencing are progressively stopped by the receding columns of the portico, and, as if to insist on the arresting movement, the vertical rectangle of the background door floats in front of the Virgin and, connecting with the dark

halo and the enveloping flow of the blue cloak, creates an ambiguity
—an abstraction of shapes culminating in a serene containment.
The control of tone and space which makes the shapes between the
figures as vital as the figures themselves demonstrates to near
perfection nearly everything that I have tried to explain about the
maintenance of the flatness, the austerity of surface which is the mark
of great monumental art. Yet despite this withdrawn quality there
is a depth of feeling about the subject which is made all the more
potent by the extreme economy with which it is produced.

We must never confuse a great work of art with the greatness or
profundity of its subject. In dealing with scale we have shown
that an over-large figure or image will reduce the greatness of a
building by setting up a scale of magnitude in opposition to that of
the environment which contains it. So it is with those artists and/or
patrons who conceive subjects of far-ranging religious or sociological
import in the belief that this will of itself produce a great window.
Dewey[1] demonstrates this distinction by contrasting the novels of
Sir Walter Scott with those of Jane Austen. The fineness of Miss
Austen's control creates a kind of organic wholeness (or form)

[1] John Dewey, *Art as Experience*. Capricorn Books, 1958, p. 17.

within the limited subject matter of social conventions of early nineteenth-century society while, with wider ranging, even ponderous, subject matter, Scott has greater difficulty in achieving any kind of form. So we must never judge a window by the scope of its subject.

14 In English windows above all, the limited, almost rustic material from which many designs are drawn lends itself to a kind of gem-like containment of formal composition, an exploitation of limited tone and colour combining with delicacy of surface treatment, which to my mind links them aesthetically to that silvery, pastoral lyricism unique to the English vision. There is nothing like it anywhere in the geography of stained glass and we do ourselves a gross injustice if, in marvelling at the grander, more dramatic windows of continental churches, we forget these quieter beauties.

Everything said so far has stressed the need for the observer's perception of design to begin with a just estimate, after a proper expenditure of time, of the demands of scale, structures, and conditions of light intrinsic to a particular architectural setting. Subject matter, in this context, is not something added to make it a superficial bit of propaganda for religion, banking, or civic pride, but is of the very fibre of the window.

This fibre will contain the artist's personal vocabulary—his symbolism or working out of images which have a special significance for him. Symbolism is another of those thorny problems. At their most superficial, symbols are nothing more than decent graphic signs, such as those used for the direction of traffic—mere reminders or signals conveying nothing of themselves but stimulating associations which are commonly understood and acted upon. In conventional public art symbols are used, and appreciated, with a perfunctoriness which amounts to no more than fingering the beads of a rosary, or a reminder to take one's mental hat off on entering a church. At the other end of the scale, symbolism may be so involved, so personal, as to be unintelligible to the viewer. An idiosyncratic language, like that of Paul Klee, does eventually communicate itself; for, as is the case with all great artists he does not wilfully seek to confuse the onlooker but rather, with the provision of keys and metaphors (such as the symbol of the eye) invites him to enter into a new world where ideas take on forms, lines, shapes, as if from some organic energy as inevitable in its growth as are those of plants and crystals. One should add, in passing, that Klee's wonderful sense of controlled activity within his private picture plane, his fresco-like feeling of impenetrable *surface* and his precise understanding of scale, make his paintings take on a monumental quality which is in line with those qualities we admire in the great fresco painters. It is no accident

Scene from tragi-comic opera, 'Sindbad the Sailor'. Paul Klee.

that many of my students have been powerfully influenced by Klee in the exploration and treatment of their experiments with personal images. In Léger's window at Audincourt the functional limitation of slab glass set in cement has led him to make quite large simple shapes—all of them based on conventional Catholic symbolism but given a fresh, almost childlike appeal. The five wounds of Christ are like four red stars and a red sun in a blue heaven and utterly remote from the bloody perforation of the human so beloved in the morbid devotions of the Counter-Reformation.

It is appropriate at this point to note that the contrasting attitudes of some of the contemporary British artists referred to in the preceding pages can be matched by their counterparts in America and on the Continent. A just evaluation of their work would require a complete chapter, not only because of the influence they have had but also on account of the far more extensive use that has been made in those countries of creative glass in architecture. I have made reference to Léger, Matisse, and Chagall, and to Robert Sowers, and it is to the last-named artist that I turn in his recent book *Stained Glass; an architectural Art* for help in getting a picture of comparative developments. In partial defence of what may appear to be highly personal opinions on my part I am bound to say that the critical position he takes seems to confirm the general thesis, namely, that the gift of true appreciation of glass in architecture does not always fall on the well-known artist or architect in other countries any more than in England. He confirms the intuitive understanding of Matisse but condemns the wilfulness of the leading of Meistermann; he applauds the 'aplomb' of Robert Lewis but is obviously unhappy with Chagall. And he instances occasions where architects have had a far better grasp of the essential scale and use of light than professional stained glass men—notably in the beautiful solution in the church of Maria Königin. We are left with the impression that because of the sheer quantity of new work that is being produced in America and in Europe a sound tradition is establishing itself, gradually winnowing out the irrelevant 'variables' of the over-publicized and the over self-assertive and settling down to a healthy anonymity of architect and artist joined in a common intention.

As with the general problem of subject matter, the use of symbolism, whether from the artist's own imagination or imposed by his patron, is only significant if it is raised to an unexpected level. The modern extensions of the human eye given us by the microscope and the camera are a new source of exploration into the infinite microcosm of nature. A sea-gull, caught by the camera in the act of landing, shows an extraordinary abstraction of the wings and tail forming several traces of the same group of feathers in different positions. It is in fact more effectively a symbol of the energy of the Holy Spirit than a representation of a smug-looking dove suspended in the clouds.

There is another type of symbolism which is nearer the poetic metaphor. By their nature such symbols defy naturalistic representation and we are forced to seek a new language of forms and colours in order to express them with something of the potency which the words conjure in the mind. In poetry many of these metaphors are purely mental. 'Or leave a kiss within the cup', immediately conveys that delicate but urgent desire for the communication of the intangible presence of the distant beloved into some present, tangible object with which he or she is associated. The metaphor remains powerful only as a verbal imagery of words and rhythm; visually it would make a rather absurd, surrealistic image. Other metaphors will stand translation into visual terms. Indeed this may develop new depths. 'The woman clothed with the sun', 'the city was pure gold, like unto clear glass', 'who is she that looketh forth as the morning, fair as the moon, clear as the sun, terrible as an army with banners?' '. . . or ever the silver cord be loosed, or the golden bowl be broken, or the pitcher be broken at the fountain, . . . then shall the dust return . . .'. These fragments from the Bible cannot be expressed in any literal sense, nor are they mere mechanical metaphors thought up by hack versifiers. They comprise a texture and rhythm of words which have embedded within them visual images which cannot be detached and depicted as a literal woman, a sun, a goldsmith's model of a city, a maiden with fancy dress heraldry, or real pitchers broken against real fountains. No artist can fully extract the ore in these deposits of poetry, but by imaginative use of semi-abstraction and, perhaps only in glass, by a full and splendid culling of light developing its own metaphysic, a true artist can restore to them their own peculiar glory. Under the strange rapture of such poetic metaphors no artist need recoil from the mention of subject matter; his chief trouble is how to translate

the obscure impulse which the subject triggers off in his mind.[1]
Something germinates for which forms must be found; the embryo
cannot be identified until the forms are found. Until the forms are
found the artist cannot know if they are the right forms, but when the
right forms are found the 'thing' is replaced by a poem or a sonata, a
painting or a sculpture. The trouble with stained glass is that such
inspired works can only come after at least one of the forms has been
established outside his control or wishes, namely the physical 'thing'
of the window itself. Even then all those other existing material
factors which we have discussed at length are bound to impinge
on whatever idea the commission has begun to conceive.

Stained glass is a horridly materialistic art—as is the religion
which gave it birth. 'Thou didst not abhor the Virgin's womb' is to
many the central stumbling block of Christian metaphysics; the
incarnation of the glazier's exalted concepts into lead and glass set
in stone is equally obstructive. When you next stand awestruck in a
cathedral and gaze up at those windows of serene jewellery, remember
how they came into the world. Think yourself into the mason's yard,
with the dusty templates, grubby rulers, arguments about the depth
of fixing grooves and positions of saddle bars; the glazier at the
bench smudged with plaster and grimed with the tarnish of lead; the
precious ruby shattered perversely against the proper fracture and
wasted; cut fingers and curses; glass half-fired or fire-cracked in a
defective kiln; the Dean and Chapter fixing an impossible date for
the great dedication service. And think yourself climbing the long,
flexing ladder to the trembling scaffolding at sixty feet above the
stone floor, rain, wind, and dust in your eyes as you struggle with a
tracery light which is too large and will not go past the cusping into
the groove. No heavenly choirs here, only the ribaldries of masons.
Yet now, seen from the floor, these voids are curtained with an
undeserved glory, light has worked a supererogation on intractable
glass and dull lead to give a tolerable glimpse of the new Jerusalem.
You should never wonder so many windows are bad, but rather
how so many manage to be so good.

[1] T. S. Eliot's *Poetry and Poets*. Faber, 1957, p. 97.

Index

movement, 108
mullions, 18
musical analogy, 65–6, 103

Nelson, Philip, 26
New, Keith, 54, 55
Newton, Eric, 98
'Nu dans la baignoire', 36

Osborne, Harold, 36
Otaniemi, Technical University, 2
Oundle School chapel, 32, 48
Oxford, Christ Church, 89

painting, 72, 74–6, ch. 8; development, 94; function and history, 81
participation, 78
Penshurst (Becket window), 35
Perpendicular style, 52
Perrot, Jean-Luc, 53
Perugino, 28
Pety family, 31
pictorial windows, 98–9, 105–6
picture making, and appreciation, 37
piece size of glass, 91
Piper, John, 48, 92, 93
plainsong, 67–8
Poitiers, 4
Pre-Raphaelite Movement, 76, 89–90
'Prick of Conscience' window, x
'Primavera', 50
Proust, Marcel, 33
Prudde, John, 31
public architecture, 95

RAF memorial window, 78, 79
Rackham, Bernard, 81
Ravenna, 28
Read, Herbert, 106n
Reformation, 5, 17
reinforced concrete, 52
religion, 10, 12, 25, 26, 34; as hindrance, 37, 38–9; and scale, 45–6
religious art, 96, 103–5
Renaissance, 28, 62
retention of the essential plane, 66–7
Reyntiens, Patrick, 92, 93
Richards, Ceri, 77

rock paintings, 64
rolled glass, 69
Ronchamp, 32
Rouault, Georges, 8, 9, 93
Rouen, 68
'Royal' window (Canterbury), 101, 110

saddle bars, 18
St. Columba, 87
St. Denis, Abbey Church, 3
St. George's, Windsor, 52
St. Gervais, life of, 68
St. Joan of Arc Church, 52, 53
St. Lorenz, Nuremberg ('Caleb and Joshua return from the promised land'), 102
St. Peter Hungate (tracery light), 11
St. Pierre, Chartres, 68
St. Stephen's Chapel, Westminster, 26
St. Urbain, Troyes, 68
Sainte-Chapelle ('chapel of glass'), 3–4
San Marco, Florence, 108–9
scale, 44–6, 48, 49–50; and line, 51–2
Schubert, Franz, 103
Sens, 4
Sèvres factory, 74
Siena, 28
'Sindbad the Sailor', 111
sound and colour, 40, 43, 61, 65–6
Sowers, Robert, 51, 87, 112
Spain, 4, 5
Spence, Sir Basil, 99
Spencer, Stanley, 108
spider's web image, 61–2
stained glass, anonymity of artists, 8; criteria, 12–13, 34; definition, 2–3, 7–8; functionalism, 9–10; geographical range, 25; sources, 3
Stained Glass; an architectural art, 112
Stamford, Connecticut ('Fish' church), iii, 32, 51, 55
stone, 51–2
subject, 39–40, 98–9, 103–5, 110; harmonization, 83–4; representation, 28, 30
surface, 61, 62, 72, 74–5, 77, 111; properties, 64, 65, 66–8, 69, 93
Swiss glass painting, 89
symbolism, 111–13